"A WIDOW-MAKING WAR"

THE LIFE AND DEATH OF A BRITISH OFFICER
IN ZULULAND, 1879

EDITED BY HOWARD WHITEHOUSE

PADDY GRIFFITH ASSOCIATES

'A Widow-Making War'
The Letters and Diaries of Major Warren Wynne RE,
edited by Howard Whitehouse
published by
PADDY GRIFFITH ASSOCIATES

First published for Lucy Wynne about 1880 – for private circulation only –
by John Adams, 49 Oxford Street, Southampton, as
MEMOIR of CAPT W R C WYNNE, R.E.
New edition 1995, by Paddy Griffith Associates,
22 Callendar Close, Nuneaton CV11 6LU

A catalogue record for this book is available from the British Library

Printed by
Warwick Printing Company Ltd

Typography by
Barrie Colwill
0151-733 3630

Front cover illustration by
Ed Dovey

Frontispiece
Wynne's grave today
Photograph by
Ian Knight

Table of Contents

List of Maps and Diagrams

Maps and Diagrams

Other Sketches and Explanations

The Dedication and Preface to the Original Collection
(published as *Memoir of Capt WRC Wynne, RE,* for private circulation only)

"The Memory of the Just is Blessed"

TO MY THREE DEAR SONS, This Memoir OF THE LAST FEW MONTHS OF
THEIR BELOVED FATHER'S LIFE IS DEDICATED BY THEIR MOTHER

In the earnest hope, and with the fervent prayer, that it may help them to know and imitate something of the true manliness, tenderness, and self-sacrificing devotion to duty which were so especially the characteristics of that DEAR FATHER, whom God in his love and wisdom removed so early from them here to meet again (God grant it!) an unbroken family in Paradise.

I feel it necessary to add a few words of explanation to the foregoing dedication. In collecting and arranging the following extracts and letters, I have chiefly had before me the desire to give to my children some record of the most memorable part of their Father's life. But it has been most difficult to do this without on the one hand publishing, though only to near relatives and friends, those loving words and messages which are to me too sacred to be read (at any rate in my lifetime) by any eyes but my own; and, on the other hand, there has been the risk of losing to my children much that would speak to them of their Father's loving thought of them, and of that spirit of strong affection for all home ties which so specially distinguished him.

I fear my effort has been but imperfectly successful; but it has been made, firstly on my children's behalf, and also with the thought of giving to those relations and friends to whom my husband was so dear some slight memorial of him.

I have not attempted to write any memoir of my Husband's earlier life, feeling that to be quite beyond my powers; and have, therefore, merely added, by way of introduction, a short biographical notice, which has already been published in a work entitled *The South African Campaign.*

LUCY WYNNE
(c.1880)

Editor's Foreword

In the autumn of 1988 Dr Paddy Griffith, then of the Department of War Studies at the Royal Military Academy Sandhurst, sent me a package and asked me to look at its contents. Inside were photocopies of a book – an old book. It contained the Letters and the Diary of a Royal Engineer officer who had served and died in the Zulu War of 1879. These two documents had been brought together in a privately printed, limited-run volume, published solely for the members of Major Warren Wynne's family sometime very soon after 1879 – probably in 1880.

Some of the material it contained appeared in the Royal Engineers' Journal at that time and Donald Morris had gained access to the Diary (or 'Journal') as a source for his monumental *The Washing of the Spears*, through Wynne's son Charles (p 623). Otherwise, neither the Letters nor the Diary have ever been available to a general audience. By chance, however, Paddy happened to be a personal friend of Margaret Wynne – the grand daughter in law of Warren Wynne – and he reported that the family has now given permission for the book to be published for a wider readership. He went on to ask whether I might be interested in editing the documents and providing a linking text. I needed no persuasion.

Major Wynne's Letters and Diary are complementary pieces, each revealing a different aspect of the writer. The Letters are addressed to his second wife, Lucy, and are charming as well as husbandly. Wynne takes time to consider details: he discusses personal feelings and plans; he observes and notes the world around him. The tone is conversational, and he engages in a real dialogue with his wife. There is much high Victorian sentimentality, and frequent reference to their shared religious faith. One cannot doubt the sincerity of Wynne's feelings, nor the longing he felt for his home and loved ones. Nevertheless Wynne did not patronise Lucy. He treated her as a partner, the mother of two of his three sons: there is no sense that he felt he had to sweeten his prose with childlike simplification.

This is not to deny that Wynne was prone to wishful thinking, or that he preferred to avoid detailing – at least at the onset – the progress of the fever that was to kill him. However his writing style is generally clear and uncluttered, without too much of the florid ornamentation so common among Victorian writers. There is a certain conversational tendency to change subjects tangentially, and to make reference to unidentified (and today – 110 years later – unidentifiable) friends and relations. Yet overall the Letters do constitute a valuable source of information – written by a man on the spot – of events that are otherwise all too little remembered or documented.

Accompanying the Letters is Wynne's Diary, covering the period from his landing in Natal in January 1879, to a moment on 11th March of that year, less than a month before his death. This is very much a professional journal – an account of an Engineer at work on a day-to-day basis. As such, it tends to emphasise detail and exactitude, rather than 'style' or any attempt at 'entertainment value'. This, after all, is its function. Paddy Griffith observed that the Diary was 'very dry & technical' in many places, and questioned whether it would be of interest to readers. My own belief, however, is that – when put into context, and supported by relevant explanation – the Diary entries lose some of their arcane 'scientific' quality. Secondly, as editor I am wary of eliminating passages of potentially interesting material – which have never before been available in print – merely because some putative non-specialist reader might be 'bored'. Wynne's daily entries of work done and plans made during the building of forts Tenedos and Eshowe, for example, are rare examples of a nineteenth century military engineer laying out and building some rather elaborate fieldworks. It would seem negligent and frivolous on my part if I were to leave aside such invaluable data, for the serious student, on the grounds that the writing was less·than Shakespearean... Thus I recommend that the reader feels free to disregard some of the overtly technical sections if it suits him or her. Perhaps at a later time they may prove to be of greater interest.

Taken together, the Letters and Diary provide a fascinating insight into the thoughts and actions of a military specialist in the Zulu War. Wynne served with Pearson's Number One Column in the coastal theatre, which was besieged at Eshowe from January to April 1879. This campaign in Eastern Zululand has received far less attention from historians than either the actions surrounding Lord Chelmsford, or the second invasion that defeated the Zulu impis outside Ulundi in July. Before the very recent work of Ian Castle and Ian Knight - *Fearful Hard Times* - there had not been a book dealing specifically with the Eshowe campaign since the 1880s, when two who had been there wrote brief accounts – Fleet-Surgeon Henry Norbury (*The Naval Brigade in South Africa during the years 1877–78–79*) and Lt Wilfrid Lloyd RA (*The Siege of Eshowe*). These are obscure works, and all efforts on my part to obtain access to them have been wholly unsuccessful to date. Wynne's writings thus fill a void by virtue of covering in detail an aspect of the war that has hitherto been largely ignored. Furthermore, happenstance dictated that in a campaign dominated by logistics and field fortifications, the Letters and Diaries are those of the key specialist officer responsible for taking many of the vital decisions.

While still on the subject of books, there have been a number of recent works comprising letters and journals of this war. In the years immediately following 1879, many officers and a handful of enlisted men wrote accounts of their own service. Some 'diaries' – such as *The War Journals of Colonel Henry Harford CB* – though useful, were heavily revised by the writer years after the war. Valuable comparisons with Wynne's letters can be found in Frank Emery's *The Red Soldier – Letters from the Zulu War, 1879*, and *Marching Over Africa*: and in Sonia Clarke's *Invasion of Zululand* and *Zululand at War*. The letters of Lt Col Arthur Harness, RA, to his family make an almost direct counterpart to Warren Wynne's letters.

For background information and references I have used a wide variety of sources, both contemporary and modern. I will not here descend to explaining the origins of my knowledge of Victorian meat extracts, ferry schedules or ditch-digging techniques; but suffice it to say that the following contemporary works proved most useful:

The Intelligence Division of the War Office, *Narrative of the Field Operations connected with the Zulu War of 1879*; and *Précis of Information Concerning Zululand*
J P MacKinnon and S H Shadbolt, *The South African Campaign of 1879*
Sir Garnet Wolseley, *The Soldier's Pocket Book for Field Service*. Twentieth century titles are variable in quality. Without attempting a thorough survey of the field, several works are worthy of special mention. Donald R Morris *The Washing of the Spears* remains the classic of the genre – a superbly complete history beginning with Shaka. More recent works have changed interpretations of several aspects of the war. Of these, J J Guy's *The Destruction of the Zulu Kingdom* is scholarly, looking at events from a Zulu perspective; while J P C Laband and P S Thompson have written several books, including the *Field Guide to the War in Zululand* and the *Defence of*

Natal and *Fight Us in the Open*. This last is an interesting collection of contemporary Zulu testimonies on the fighting. The Victorian Military Society published a short selection of recent articles in *There Will Be An Awful Row At Home About This*. Ian Knight's *The Zulus* is also a fine brief work, largely superseding Angus McBride's *The Zulu War*. Among general histories, David Clammer's *The Zulu War*, and Michael Barthorp's *The Zulu War, a Pictorial History*, are concise and accessible. Lastly, I would add that the experience of writing my *Battle in Africa 1879–1914* (Fieldbooks, 1988) helped me to analyse the general problems of campaigning in African conditions during these years.

I have tried to be consistent in spelling Zulu and Afrikaans names, using generally accepted forms where possible, even these are not always 'pure', 'Inyezane, for example, is more usually called simply 'Nyezane' today. Thus the place that Wynne knew as 'Ekowe', and others as 'Etschowi' or even 'Tyoë', is referred to as 'Eshowe'. Wynne's 'Cetewayo' is given here as 'Cetshwayo'.

I owe grateful thanks to a number of people, amongst them –

The Wynne family, for their generous co-operation with this project.
Ms Beverley Williams, Assistant Curator of the Royal Engineers Museum at Chatham, for valuable data on service records, organisation, and some of the more arcane aspects of engineering science.
The staff of the Maud M Burrus Library in Decatur, Georgia, for their patience in receiving requests for obscure books and pamphlets, on a regular and frequent basis.
Warner Stark, for gaining access to technical works via the US Army library system.
James Atwood for his advice on fortification techniques.
Shuter & Shooter Ltd, of Pietermartizburg, for kind permission to quote from *Fight us in the open*.
Nicola Porter for her excellent typing.
Ian Knight for generous help on a number of fronts.
Special thanks go to Peter Dennis and Paddy Griffith of Fieldbooks, for their own contributions to this book; and especially to my wife – Lori Knight-Whitehouse – for her encouragement of my work, and her toleration of my working habits.

Howard Whitehouse, Decatur, May 1989

Glossary of Terms and Abbreviations

AAG   Assistant Adjutant General

Adjutant   a senior officer within a military force, responsible for discipline and drill

AQMG   Assistant Quarter Master General

Banquette   Infantry fire step, located just behind a fortress rampart

Caponier   Blockhouse in a fortress ditch, to give flanking fire within it

CB   Companion of the Bath (= an order of chivalry)

CRE   'Commander of Royal Engineers' in a particular force

DAG   Deputy Adjutant General

DAQMG   Deputy Assistant Quarter Master General

Drift   Ford or river crossing

Fascines   bundles of branches or heavy reeds, used in engineering work for filling in ditches &c.

Glacis   Open ground, without cover, sloping up to a fortress all around it

GOC   General Officer Commanding

Ibutho   Zulu Regiment of no fixed size. The plural is Amabutho

Impi   a Zulu Armed Force (not necessarily a regiment)

KCB   Knight Commander of the Bath

Kloof   Hollow or ravine, often wooded, in the Dutch frontier dialect that would become Afrikaans

NNC   Natal Native Contingent

Pr   'Pounder': ie the definition of a cannon by the weight of its shell (eg a '7 pr' is a gun that fires a shell weighing seven pounds)

RA   Royal Artillery

RGA   Royal Garrison Artillery

RE   Royal Engineers

Regiments of Foot mentioned in the narrative:-

     2nd: The Royal West Surrey Regiment (The Queen's)

     3rd: The Kentish Regiment (Buffs):

     4th: The Royal Lancaster Regiment (King's Own)

     24th: The South Wales Borderers (formerly 2nd Warwickshire Regt)

     29th: The Worcestershire Regiment

     32nd: The Duke of Cornwall's Light Infantry

91st: The Argyll and Sutherland Highlanders (Princess Louise's)
99th: The Wiltshire Regiment (Duke of Edinburgh's)
103rd: The Royal Bombay Fusiliers

RMA   Royal Military Academy, Woolwich (for gunners and engineers, as opposed to the Royal Military College at Sandhurst. In 1947 the two schools were amalgamated, at Sandhurst).

Reveillé   The formal military moment for waking up a sleeping force

Revetment Retaining wall, or outer covering of solid material placed over an earthwork to keep it in place & protected from the elements

RNR   Royal Navy Reserve

Introduction – An Officer of Engineers

About 1880 Lucy Parish Wynne sat down to write a short biography of her husband, who had died the previous year in South Africa. It was to be published as an obituary in Shadbolt and MacKinnon's compilation, *The South African Campaign, 1879*. This volume was to feature a cabinet photograph and a brief remembrance of every officer who had fallen in the Zulu War. Many of these individuals had been killed at the disastrous battle of Isandhlwana; others in lesser actions both lost and won. A significant number of them, however, had died not on what the romantics chose to call 'The Field of Valour'; but of fatigue, accident or fever.

Warren Wynne was one of this group. Officers who die of overwork and sickness generally receive less attention than those who fall transfixed by fire and steel; and those who serve in secondary theatres, without benefit of glorious victories or catastrophic defeats, get even less. Thus most of what is known of Wynne derives from his wife's brief sketch of his life. This begins as follows:-

§ Major Warren Richard Colvin Wynne, who died at Fort Pearson on the Natal Frontier, on the 9th April 1879, was the eldest surviving son of Captain John Wynne, Royal Horse Artillery, of Wynnestay, County Dublin, by his marriage with Anne, daughter of Admiral Sir Samuel Warren, KCB, GCH. He was born on the 9th April, 1843, at Collon House, County Louth, and was educated at the Royal Naval School, New Cross, where he carried off numerous prizes, including two silver medals for Classics and Mathematics. He passed out from the Royal Military Academy, Woolwich, fourth on the list of successful candidates, and elected to serve in the Royal Engineers. On the 25th June, 1862, he was gazetted to a Lieutenancy in this corps. His first foreign service was at Gibraltar, where he remained for five years, and was appointed Acting Adjutant, an appointment he held for four years. On his return to England he was appointed to the Ordnance Survey in December, 1871, and stationed at Guildford, from whence he was removed to Reading in November 1875. In December, 1878, at a day's notice, he was given the command of the 2nd Field Company, then stationed at Shorncliffe, and under orders to proceed on active service to Natal, in view of the impending invasion of Zululand.

At this point Lucy Wynne provided a summary of her husband's service in the Zulu War, and an assessment of the value of his work, quoting extensively from brother officers who had served alongside him. For the purposes of the present book, some of these comments have been removed to the final chapter.

Lucy ends the biography with a note regarding herself:-

The Family Tree of Warren Wynne

The Wynne family originated in Merioneth. Colonel Owen Wynne of Bala, North Wales, was a Law Commissioner (supply) for Cromwell in Ireland. He was rewarded with land and established the branch of the family from which Warren was descended (d1670/71). The next four generations in direct line all joined the army, including Capt Owen Wynne, c.1686–1757, who campaigned with Marlborough; and Lt Col Owen Wynn MP, who died in 1789)

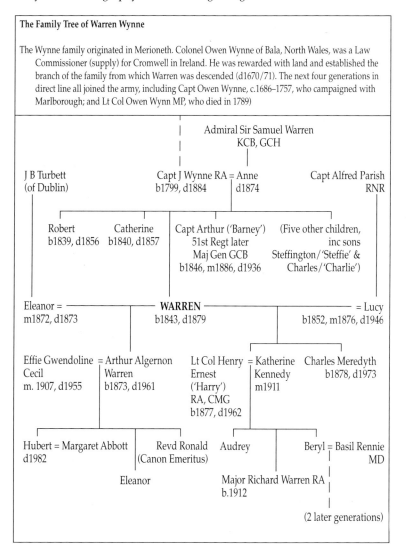

Admiral Sir Samuel Warren
KCB, GCH

J B Turbett
(of Dublin)

Capt J Wynne RA = Anne
b1799, d1884   d1874

Capt Alfred Parish
RNR

Robert
b1839, d1856

Catherine
b1840, d1857

Capt Arthur ('Barney')
51st Regt later
Maj Gen GCB
b1846, m1886, d1936

(Five other children,
inc sons
Steffington/'Steffie' &
Charles/'Charlie')

Eleanor =
m1872, d1873

WARREN
b1843, d1879

= Lucy
b1852, m1876, d1946

Effie Gwendoline = Arthur Algernon
Cecil   Warren
m. 1907, d1955   b1873, d1961

Lt Col Henry = Katherine
Ernest   Kennedy
('Harry')   m1911
RA, CMG
b1877, d1962

Charles Meredyth
b1878, d1973

Hubert = Margaret Abbott
d1982

Revd Ronald
(Canon Emeritus)

Eleanor

Audrey

Major Richard Warren RA
b.1912

Beryl = Basil Rennie
MD

(2 later generations)

¶ Major Wynne was twice married: first, in 1872, to Eleanor, seventh daughter of J B Turbett, Esq, of Owenstown, Dublin (who died in 1873); and secondly, in 1876, to Lucy, eldest daughter of Captain Alfred Parish, RNR.

Other sources tell us little more of the man. He was, like many other officers of the Victorian army, born in Ireland, of a military family founded by one of Cromwell's men. The Anglo-Irish gentry formed a proud, protestant, often penniless squirearchy which provided a conspicuously successful element in the officer corps. Wolseley, Kitchener and Roberts – Kipling's 'Bobs' – were all products of this class.

Wynne's father had been a soldier; his grandfather a Navy man – so there were traditional demands on the young Warren. But despite the bias of his education towards the Senior Service, he chose to take the entrance exam for the Royal Military Academy ('The Shop') at Woolwich. His academic achievements at school had been unusual, and in most Victorian families of the upper classes a bright boy would have been diverted away from a military career, into Law or Government. However, the militant Irish gentry held soldiering in high esteem, and the sons of officers were not accorded much of a choice. Wynne passed into 'The Shop', and continued to apply himself to his studies. The RMA boasted that it existed to nourish the best brains in the army – and certainly the competition for a place was fierce. The RMA trained officers for 'the technical services' – the Artillery and Engineers – and those who completed the two-and-a-half year course received a free commission as a lieutenant.

The course was challenging. The 'Gentleman Cadet' had to study not only the scientific aspects of Gunnery and Engineering – with a bias towards Calculus and Geometry – but also Fortification and Bridging; Natural and Experimental Philosophy, and Landscape Drawing. There were lectures on Astronomy, Mineralogy, Metallurgy and Geology. Aside from these sciences, there were languages – French, German and Hindustani – and the physical exercise of Fencing and Riding. There was also, of course, the military ritual of Foot Drill, at regular and frequent intervals.

There were around 200 cadets at any one time, with a drastically varying number in each graduating class. Thus when Louis Napoleon, the French Prince Imperial, passed out of Woolwich in 1875, he stood seventh in a list of 35. Traditionally the top ten cadets had the privilege of entering the Royal Engineers; the rest going into the less prestigious Artillery. Sometimes the

Sappers had more vacancies – in 1868 John Chard, the future hero of Rorke's Drift, scraped into the Royal Engineers as the eighteenth of nineteen new commissions. Hence Wynne's own high placing – he graduated fourth in his class – entirely guaranteed him a posting to the Engineers; and he took it.

Some two centuries before Warren Wynne took up his commission, the Royal Engineers had originated as a corps of officers governed by the Board of Ordnance. They specialised in the technical areas of Fortification and Siegecraft; Surveying; Road Building, and related duties. An auxiliary body of enlisted personnel – variously known as the Royal Military Artificers, and later the Royal Sappers and Miners – was raised in 1787. After the Crimean War the Board of Ordnance was abolished, and the RE was re-organised as a corps consisting of all ranks. During the Victorian period the Sappers remained responsible for their traditional spheres of expertise – but added new types of military activity such as Explosive Demolition, Ballooning, Signals & Telegraphy, Military Railways and Photography. One engineer defined his role as 'A man of all work for the Army and the Public... ready to do anything and go anywhere'.

Warren Wynne was in many ways ideally cut-out for the Royal Engineers. He was an intelligent man with a keen eye for detail – devoted to his work; meticulous, and a perfectionist. His letters from Zululand show no interest in the passing glories of war; but rather a compelling urge to do not only what was needed – but what was the best. He was irked by negligence and bad planning, but was loyally silent on the manifest failings of his superiors. The training at Woolwich was designed to produce skilled technicians rather than gallant leaders of men. Dashing cavaliers – the high-sprited young bloods who lived for the hounds, London society, and expensive, raucous evenings of Claret and wagering – were not welcome in the Royal Engineers; and they in turn were generally uninterested in the steady, unglamorous life of the Sapper.

Wynne's career was not an untypical one. He had enjoyed one foreign posting prior to the Zulu War; in the quiet, well-established garrison of Gibraltar. He displayed the stable, reliable character that made him Acting Adjutant within a year of his arrival there. He then served for seven years in the quasi-civilian role of Ordnance Surveyor. Promotion was by seniority, and slow. He was made up to Captain only in February 1875 – after almost twelve years as a Lieutenant – and would become a Major only in April 1879, 'In recognition of his distinguished services' in South Africa, precisely one week before his death.

In an army where most officers were bachelors, or married late, he was twice-wedded; the first time as a Lieutenant of twenty nine years. This was highly unusual, since the common service wisdom was that – 'While Captains might marry, Majors should, and Colonels must; but Lieutenants

---

Officers of the Royal Engineers

Officers of the Royal Engineers played a prominent role in the Zulu War of 1879. Some were employed in the traditional duties of the military engineer, while others found themselves in situations outside the general run of their training and experience.

Lt Col Anthony William Durnford had served in Ceylon, Malta and Gibraltar, but had seen no war service when he arrived in South Africa at the age of forty one in 1871. He lost an arm in a disastrous action against the Hlubi chieftain Langalibalele, where his outspoken criticism of local volunteer troops made him the obvious scapegoat for the failure of the operation – at least as far as Natal was concerned. Impulsive, highly-strung and a natural gambler, Durnford was given command of the reserve Number Two Column at the outbreak of the Zulu campaign in 1879, so that Lord Chelmsford could keep a check on his independence. However, he was ordered up to Isandhlwana on January 22nd, where he found himself in command. Durnford's share of responsibility for the catastrophic defeat remains a subject of debate; but it is clear that he fought bravely and fell during a gallant last stand.

Lt John Rouse Merriott Chard was commissioned in 1868, and served in Malta and Bermuda before going out to Natal with the 5th Field Company in December 1878. At thirty two he was still awaiting his first promotion, and did not seem destined to great things. He was considered 'hopelessly slow and slack' by his commanding officer, and was put in charge of the punts across the Buffalo River at Rorke's Drift. On 22nd January, as senior officer there, he commanded the garrison of less than 100 fit men against the onslaught of some 4,000 Zulus. In the acclaim for the successful defence, Chard was awarded the Victoria Cross, promoted to Major – jumping the rank of Captain – and was invited to Balmoral by the Queen. His subsequent career did not prosper, however, and after service in Cyprus, India and Singapore he retired as a Lieutenant Colonel in 1897, three months before he died of cancer.

Col Fairfax Charles Hassard CB was the Commander of Royal Engineers in South Africa, an officer with forty years' service. He was not, however, well suited for his position – being 'rather old for such work'.[1] After the Isandhlwana débâcle he was placed in command of the frontier zone south of Rorke's Drift... 'So, Royal Engineer-like, he built a fort at Helpmekaar, and shut himself up in it, and strongly recommended everyone else to do the same'.[2]

Lt Col Richard Harrison had no experience of either staffwork or of South Africa, when he was appointed Assistant Adjutant and Quartermaster General on May 5th, 1879. In that role he was judged partially to blame for the death of the Prince Imperial, son of the French Emperor Napoleon III, on a reconnaissance patrol on 2nd June. Harrison's comrades in the field, however, came to consider him 'a most excellent officer'.[3] He commanded the Flying Column after Evelyn Wood went home, and became military commander in the Transvaal at the end of the war.

Lt J C MacGregor was in charge of the signal stations between Durban and Ulundi; he served against Sekukuni, and was killed at Ingogo in the first Boer War. **Lt Walter James** was a staff officer in the last stages of the war before retiring to become a military 'crammer' for examination candidates, and writing an account of the Waterloo campaign. **Captain Walter Parke Jones**, and his subordinate, Lt Charles Commeline, wrote a series of valuable letters home, which are collected in Frank Emery's two books.

Establishment of an RE Field Company, 1877[4]				
–Officers & Men Field Company	Mounted	Dismounted	**Horses & Carriages Fld Co.**	
Officers:			*Horses:*	
Major	1		Officer Private	2
Captain	1		Public	9
Lieutenant	3		NCO	3
Surgeon	1		Trumpeters	1
TOTAL:	**6**		Store Wagons	24
			Pack Eqpt.	3
Other Ranks:			Spare	4
Sergeants	1	6	'Wagons, Store'	6
Corporals	1	6	TOTAL:	52
2nd Corporal	1	6		
Shoeing Smith	1			
Sappers		134		
Drivers	26		*Small Arms:*	
Trumpeters	1		Rifles	152
Buglers		1	Sword bayonet	1
Batmen		12	Cavalry sword	6
TOTAL:	**37**	165	Pistols	1
Cartridges				
Per man: Rifle		50		
Pistol		24		

It is apparent that Wynne's company was seriously understrength, at 125 all ranks, despite recent recruiting. As a Captain, he was himself below rank for the command.

The Sappers in this 'ideal company' were designated according to their specialist duties; Carpenters (32) and Masons (28) made up the largest groups; but there were also Smiths, Clerks, Bricklayers, Painters, Smiths, Tailors, Miners, Wheelwrights and Coopers, Collar Makers, Telegraphists – and one solitary Printer & Photographer. A breakdown of the company's transport shows three store wagons – one each for camping, 'office' and tentage – and a forge... each drawn by four horses. These arrangements, of course, could not be strictly applied on campaign in South Africa, where conditions dictated the use of locally-found vehicles and draught animals – primarily oxen.

definitely should not.' The married soldier had - it was said - two loyalties, and would not engage wholeheartedly in the life of his regiment. There was probably less concern about this in the RE than in other branches of the services – but Wynne's case was still, perhaps, exceptional.

Wynne's photograph *(used as the basis for the front cover portrait)*, shows a youngish man in half-profile, apparently slight of build. He has short fair hair, glossed carefully down – no side whiskers (which were enjoying a lastgasp of popularity in military fashion) - but an impressive drooping moustache. The nose is large – obviously so – but there is a gentleness to the eyes and mouth. The expression is earnest and, dressed in civilian clothes, he resembles a Presbyterian Minister rather than a Son of Mars. Indeed, it is hard to imagine Warren Wynne – devoted husband, doting father of three sons, a man of deep religious convictions – engaged in the typical activities of the young officer; sabre-rattling over the port, or riding a hunter around the stacked furniture of the Mess. Wynne wished merely to do his duty and then return home; that he was never to do.

References

1) Lt Col Arthur Harness RA, in Clarke's *Invasion of Zululand* pp 92–3
2) Major C F Clery, 32nd Regiment, in Clarke's *Zululand at War* p 133
3) Lt Col C E East, 57th Regiment, Ibid p 259
4) Taken from D E Langley *The Organisation of the British Army*, in Knight's *Awful Row* p 36

Chapter One: Shorncliffe Camp - Preparing for War

In November 1878, the word was that war was expected in South Africa. Correspondence from Sir Bartle Frere, governor of Cape Colony, indicated that hostilities between Britain and the Zulu nation were likely to break out at any time. The Colonial Secretary, the ineffectual Sir Michael Hicks Beach, considered each letter from Frere with mounting apprehension. With a war already in Afghanistan – and the Balkans in turmoil – London was not at all happy that a headstrong proconsul, in what was only a second-string colony, should be playing a gambler's risk for uncertain stakes.

The jumbled origins of the Zulu crisis extend far back to the original Dutch seizure of the Cape of Good Hope in the Seventeenth century. This was followed by a successful British invasion during the Napoleonic Wars, and soon afterwards by a period of violent Zulu expansionism further North under Shaka (who died in 1828). The Great Trek of the Boers in 1834 put the Dutch settlers beyond the reach of Crown authority; but their subsequent land-taking to the North had the unfortunate effect of placing them in direct confrontation with the Zulus.

The Afrikaners had veered away from the coastal lowlands towards the high, bare veldt above the Drakensburg mountains. British settlement in Natal, on the other hand, had been slower and less hostile to the Zulus. The latter saw the Crown as an ally – albeit a lukewarm one – against the hated Dutch. As the Zulus settled down under their passive king mPande (1840–72), it appeared that the ripples, created in the tumultuous period of Zulu conquest and Boer expansion, were fading at last. Sir Bartle Frere, however, had his own personal pebble to lob.

Britain was not inclined to allow her unwilling, Dutch-speaking subjects simply to hike off into the interior, and in 1877 the crown annexed the bankrupt Boer republics of the Transvaal and the Orange Free State. Frere was an advocate of 'Confederation' which linked the former Boer states with the older British colonies – a plan that was to sink without trace in 1880–1, when the Transvaalers took back their independence by force.

At the close of 1878 the scheme nevertheless still had some life in it – but the problem was that it unexpectedly led to a sudden switch in Britain's 'Native Policy'. Boer relations with Africans had never been good, and the Zulus were by now an historic enemy of the Transvaalers. The early Trekkers had encroached on Zulu territory in their attempt to settle in Natal, and had defeated the Zulus at Blood River in 1838. They remained interested in exploiting Zulu land and labour, which meant that independent Zululand was always a likely target for armed intervention. By annexing the Boers, therefore, Britain gratuitously and unintentionally took over a long–standing 'cold war' with the Zulus.

The paradoxical result of annexation was that the Boers could now call on their new British suzerains for aid against the Zulus. The Zulu state, once seen by the British as a useful counterweight to Transvaal ambitions, now appeared to Frere as a dangerous, unstable – and of course 'savage' – obstacle to progress. After all, Her Majesty's Government was not traditionally tolerant of neighbours who declined to take British advice or offer proper subservience.

Recent historians have rightly questioned the position of Frere, and have seen him as sowing dissent where otherwise peace might have reigned. He was new to Africa, something of a zealot, and had persuaded himself that the Zulus were about to invade British territory of their own accord. He determined to launch a pre-emptive attack. Some minor border incidents involving King Cetshwayo's defiantly traditional values concerning justice and retribution, together with a long-standing land dispute between Transvaalers and Zulus, became the excuse for Frere's military solution. He took a policy of informing London only when it suited him, and his demands for reinforcements from the vacillating Hicks Beach served only to increase the pace of developments.

In November the authorities in London agreed to send more troops to South Africa, among them the 2nd Field Company of Royal Engineers, commanded by Captain Wynne.

Warren Wynne had been slung in at the proverbial 'deep end'. With only a day's notice, he took the train from Eastbourne along the coast to Sandgate in Kent, to take charge of his first command. The circumstances which required that the 2nd Field Company should receive a new commanding officer with such haste are not recorded. The timing was certainly not propitious, for the process of mobilising a unit was never easy. Engineer

THE ZULU ARMY OF 1879

The Zulu nation had been the most powerful military and political force in Bantu Africa since the time of Shaka, the founder of a military system which had allowed them to grow from a small group of clans to conquer or drive away their neighbours in a brief, devastating period known as the mFecane - 'The Time of the Crushing'. In 1879, at the time of King Cetshwayo (or 'Cetewayo' to Wynne), the Zulu army comprised some 55,000 men in 33 regiments, of which perhaps 40,000 were of fighting age. The army was essentially a militia of all adult males, formed into 'age-set' regiments, varying in size from a few hundred (eg the mBube, iQwa and nKhonkhone) to the huge, young 'amabutho' such as the unCijo (c. 9,000 strong) and the nGomabakosi (c. 6,000). The key division was between the unmarried 'amabutho', of bachelors forbidden to wed until they had 'washed their spears' in enemy blood, and the privileged married units who wore a distinctive headring. While the single men lived in communal military kraals, the married warriors were permitted to establish independent family lives. All, however, could be called upon at any time for war service. The system meant that there was a continuing pressure for war, to let the young warriors marry – a pressure that was exploited by British proponents of intervention. Cetshwayo was aware of the issue, and made efforts to defuse the martial and marital impulses of his bachelor regiments.

Zulu tactics were aggressive: they had no interest in defensive methods, and no real capacity for them. Instead, the Zulus refined the envelopment tactics traditional to the African peoples. The Zulus were brave and fleet of foot – but so were other tribes. What Shaka gave his army was twofold. First he developed discipline and organisation, with a rank structure, uniform shields and costume, and a set position for each man in his 'iVivo' or company. Secondly, Shaka abandoned the old throwing spear, with its emphasis on inconclusive skirmishing, for a fearsome broad-bladed stabbing assegai, known as the 'Ikhlwa'. Used in combination with the shield, this made a potent close-quarter combination. The army was divided into four parts for battle, likened to a charging bull. The two 'horns' encircled; the 'chest' came to the assault, while the reserve – usually composed of veteran units – held back from the fray. Battles were generally quick and decisive. Although many Zulus had firearms, usually obsolete muskets acquired by trade or in payment for work, most had little skill or understanding of their proper use. Accounts of the 1879 campaign often refer to heavy but ineffective Zulu fire. The focus remained on the all-out assault and the commanding 'Indunas', who scouted the ground and directed the action from selected vantage points, were often faced with the problem of holding their men in check. At Isandhlwana, Kambula and Ulundi, the central direction of the battle fell apart as the impis simply rushed headlong into the attack.

---

companies were burdened with tons of specialist equipment, and so were especially prone to embed themselves into the fabric of established stations. Not surprisingly, Wynne was scarcely encouraged by his first day of duty:

¶ 'Shorncliffe Camp, 29th November, 1878 – Everything here is in the most awful state of confusion. The authorities have given orders and counter-orders to such an extent that there is no knowing how to turn. We are to embark on Monday; I expect Monday afternoon will be the time for your Father and Charlie to come. I have just had a parade of my Company; they are good specimens on the whole, but even yet we have not got our numbers. There have been so many changes, which of course make things difficult to work. I find it very difficult to get any tangible grasp of the organisation and equipment of the company. I sincerely hope you will be able to come out before long – from the little I have been able to glean, I should say there will not be likely to be anything to prevent it.[1]'

Shorncliffe Camp had been established in 1803 and soon became the site of Sir John Moore's famous training centre for the light infantry. It was here that the Light Division – Wellington's crack formation in the Peninsular War – learned its trade. Shorncliffe was built on high ground to the north of the coastal town of Sandgate, some three miles west of Folkestone. It had a useful strategic position in case of French invasion; but by 1879 it was an ageing facility, laid out in rows of wooden huts rather than the large barrack blocks which characterised so many other, newer, Victorian military posts.

¶ 'Shorncliffe, November 30th – I have indeed had a hard bewildering time of it since my arrival here yesterday morning. I feel quite dazed with all the multitude of business; telegrams pouring in by twos and threes at a time, requiring immediate answers and necessitating work, work, work. Then at this juncture they have exchanged the Company Pay Sergeant for a new man, who has to become initiated in everything, and therefore the man one most wants is unavailable. I got to bed at 11.30pm last night, having had no meal but my early breakfast at Charing Cross[2]. I managed to get two or three sandwiches from the Guards' Mess; these and your sandwiches formed my only meals all day. Last night was bitterly cold in the hut, and prevented my sleeping well, but I am in spite of all none the worse in health thank God, and when once we are embarked I expect I shall get on grandly. To-day I made a point of getting breakfast and lunch at the Artillery Mess, and having found an old kettle, have made myself some Liebig,[3] and later on some tea in my hut. I shall not dine at Mess, as I must get time to write a few private letters, in addition to the Company work. We shall have plenty to do up to the time we sail, and no end of organisation when we get out to S. Africa. I hope I shall get all settled pretty well before you come out. The Company will be split up into several sections and distributed along a long line of frontier,[4] and I shall probably be pretty stationary at some head-quarters... We were inspected to-day by the Commandant of the Garrison. The Company made a respectable appearance, 125 strong. I think I told you it was to perform a regular tour of foreign service.[5] To-morrow, alas! will be anything but a day of rest – there is work to do nearly all day, and no church parade. We have to load railway vans with the remainder of the luggage in the afternoon, because our start the next morning at 6.30am will be too early, and it will be too dark to do any baggage loading, etc. We shall arrive at Gravesend about 11.15am and be embarked at mid-day Monday, so I hope Father and Charlie will be able to come that afternoon. We shall start next day. The *Walmer Castle* is one of Donald Currie & Co's mail steamers, so I hope we shall be pretty comfortable. I shall get to church at some time or other to-morrow. I cannot miss the last chance in England for so long. I hope it will be the morning service.'

Wynne hurled himself into combat against the bureaucracy, routine and inertia that worked to immobilise the Victorian army. His energy and perfectionism were needed, fortime was short and key administrative personnel were notable by their absence. Fortunately, as he was to discover, the company was blessed with a capable group of subalterns. The senior lieutenant, David Charles Courtney, had been in the corps for twelve years and was expecting his Captaincy at any time. If there was any ill-feeling at being passed over for command, Courtney never showed any sign of it. Probably he knew that a more senior man was bound to get the job.

Lieutenant Harry Borlase Willock had received his commission in 1872, and would later serve in Wolseley's 1882 expedition to Egypt. The junior man was Charles Hayes, commissioned in 1875. These officers had overseen the training of young recruits to fill out the ranks for field service.

¶ 'Shorncliffe Camp, 1st December, 1878 – It is now past 7pm. I have been at work incessantly all day, and have some more Company business to attend to by-and-by - such a Sunday! How I longed to be with you to enjoy quiet and peace. I was utterly unable to get to church in the morning, but hoped to go to evening service, and now I have missed that. To-day has been miserably wet. I hope it may clear by to-morrow morning. We officers breakfast with Colonel Duff, CRE, who has been very kind, at 6.15am, and march off from the camp at 7.15 for Sandgate Station. I hope all my arrangements for the orderly conveyance of the men by railway etc. will prove satisfactory, and also that the predicted gale for the 3rd may not be realised, and make the poor fellows wretchedly sea sick. We take the women and children, but I believe they are intended not to go further than Durban. We are taking out an enormous quantity of baggage.[6] I was absolutely obliged to send the last of it to-day, as our start to-morrow is so early and dark. I have nothing left but my camp bedstead, great coat, and waterproof; these will go in the morning.'

1) The hope that Lucy would be able to come out to South Africa was not to be fulfilled – for her or for any other officer's wives – but the prospect was undoubtedly a great comfort to Wynne.
2) Charing Cross is, of course, a major railway station in central London.
3) 'Liebig' was a brand of meat extract used as a spread or for making 'beef tea'.
4) This did not happen. The 2nd Field Company served as a complete unit throughout the Zulu War.
5) No record remains of the intended destination of the company.
6) The precise amount of equipment required for a company of engineers varied according to local needs and circumstances. However, merely the tents and other camping stores for a company weighed about a ton – more when wet.

Chapter Two: The 'Walmer Castle' - Life Aboard a Troop Transport

The embarkation of troops was a complicated operation. The British army, which was notoriously lacking in arrangements for almost every military necessity, had copious regulations for the transit of its forces by sea. An officer's cabin allowance was 195 cubic feet, or 270 if two officers shared. This was rather more generous than the 52 cubic feet for a private soldier or, indeed, 126 for a horse. The regulations emphasised the need for detailed examination of the ship for sanitary facilities and ventilation; the discipline of the troops, and – especially – the care of the horses. The whole procedure was likely to be confused and noisy. Wynne's letter, written on 2nd December, reflects this chaos – as well as his own discomfort at his unfamiliar responsibilities at this time.

¶ 'SS WALMER CASTLE, 2nd December – I will write again in the hope of being able to get this taken ashore by the pilot. I was bitterly disappointed not to have seen Father and Charlie before we left. In the midst of all this horrid confusion and noise, and one's miserable state of nervelessness, after days and nights of hurried work, it would indeed have been a consolation and refreshment to have seen their loved faces, and got a hearty hand-shake, and cheering word from them. I am afraid I am in the dismals. The British soldier is a fine fellow, but you may have too much of him. My own men are very well, exceptionally so, but the others with us are a very rough lot, and the most horrible oaths are sounding around one. What a Sunday I had yesterday. After I finished my letter to you last night, I had to set to work again, and was constantly at it till 1.30 this morning, having to be up again at 5.15. I had, necessarily, parted with nearly all bedding and wraps, so was chilly, and got but little sleep, so you may be sure I shall be glad of a little rest and quiet at sea; though, of course, one will not be left idle, there will be duty in one's turn with the troops... They have certainly lost no time in getting us off, in spite of the Queen's regulations, which require twenty-four hours' delay after embarkation.[1] We left Shorncliffe at 7.15 a.m., played down by the fifes and drums of the Guards, and the band of the 45th, and arrived on board at 1.30. There are four or five ladies of the 99th Regiment with us. I suppose they will stop at Durban. The accounts I hear of the Cape seem in general terms to resolve themselves into 'rough, unluxurious, and very healthy – summer heat, not troublesome on account of cool nights. ' We are to call at Madeira and Cape Town, so I must send you good budgets from those places. We have just anchored opposite Sheerness, as we have to take powder on board to-morrow. How provoking that we should be waiting here instead of at Gravesend, for then I might have seen Father and Charlie. I suppose I had better now wish you a happy Christmas, for a letter from Madeira might not reach you in time. I wish you and all the dear ones with you a very happy Christmas, and you may be sure my thoughts will be with you on that day.'

The Walmer Castle was one of a fleet of vessels, all bearing the suffix 'Castle', belonging to Donald Currie and Company. Their 'Castle Line' served the Cape Town route, and was assigned to carry the Royal Mail. Several of the Walmer Castle's sister ships – including the *Dunrobin*, *Dublin* and *Edinburgh Castles* – were also engaged by HM Government to transport men and supplies to South Africa.

¶ 'SS WALMER CASTLE, 3rd December – As we have a parade at 10am, and I shall probably be kept on duty for some time after, I must make sure of writing a few lines to be ready for the pilot. It was such a pleasure to see Father and Charlie after all, and so good of them to take such trouble to come down to the ship off Sheerness. It did cheer me up to see their faces, and it will be satisfactory to you to have their report of me. I had a splendid sleep last night, and all is going on well. I hope, in about a fortnight, you may hear from Madeira.'

Sheerness was, and is, a town on the north coast of the Isle of Sheppey, in the Thames estuary. In 1878 it was a garrison town with naval repair facilities. If Wynne's father-in-law had any difficulty in making arrangements to travel out to the *Walmer Castle*, no doubt his naval connections would have helped him to get his wish.

¶ 'SS WALMER CASTLE, 11th December, 1878 – I must now take up my diary letter, from the date of our arrival at Madeira, viz: Sunday, the 8th inst. We had a good view of the east side of the island, the outline of which struck me as being very picturesque. The tints upon the hill sides, the greys, purples, russet browns, and emerald, were such as promised, in bright sunshine, to be very lovely. As it was, there was a good deal of heavy mist which shortly turned into heavy rain, and somewhat detracted from the effect; the sea was too rough, making large white surf along the beach. We were, most of us, determined however to go ashore in spite of any difficulties. So first one boat with nine officers, and then another with eight, and one of the ladies, put off for the shore. I was in the second. It required a certain amount of quickness to effect a landing without being drenched by the surf, and the lady needed strong nerve and the help of four men to get from the boat on to the landing place. It was now 12.30pm, too late for Divine Service, and they had none on board, on account of coaling etc., so it was a second Sunday for me without any. How sadly one will now miss the blessings of such a place of worship as we experienced at Reading. It is only by the loss that one realises the preciousness of it. I was pleased with what I saw of Madeira. We only had a bare three hours there, and one longed for a fine day and seven or eight hours to be able to explore some of the tempting looking ravines and summits of the island. As it was, it never ceased raining while we were there, and we could only walk through and about the town of Funchal. It is clean as foreign towns go, neatly paved with pitcher paving. The conveyances for passengers are peculiar, being light basket carriages on wooden frames like sleighs, iron shod, with a four-poster arrangement closed around with curtains. These are drawn by a pair of bullocks, which go at a very fair pace along the paved streets. At 3.30, we returned to the ship, and left Madeira in a storm of rain, wind, thunder, and lightning, at 5pm, the band of *HMS Boadicea* striking up Auld Lang Syne, as we steamed off.'

The need to take on coal was a central theme in the maritime affairs of this period. British naval policy was largely built around coaling stations, and many of the crown's overseas possessions were founded from this requirement. Madeira belonged to Britain's ancient ally Portugal, and owed much of its meagre prosperity to its strategic position off the coast of West Africa, directly on the steamer routes. The coaling operation was in the hands of two local companies.

Madeira was a volcanic island, with the kind of geological features that a surveyor would have appreciated. It produced sugar and wine, supporting a fairly dense population of mixed Portuguese/African stock. The principal town was Funchal, which was well regarded by Wynne. Until the submarine cable reached Cape Town in the next few years, Madeira was the closest telegraphic link to South Africa from Europe.

¶ '15th, Sunday – To-day is rather more like Sunday than the last two; but now little like our delightful Sundays together at Reading. We had service on the quarter-deck at 10.30am. The Captain of the ship read the service, and the hymns were fairly sung. We shall, I suppose, spend our next Sunday but one at Cape Town, for I do not think we shall arrive there till the Saturday after Christmas Day. Then there will be another four or five days before reaching Durban, by which time I for one will be heartily tired of the voyage. The last fortnight seems like three months at least. I am so very anxious to hear how the Afghan expedition is progressing, especially Arthur's[2] column. I wonder whether the papers at home will have accounts of our little campaign.

The fellows talk of a Zulu War Medal, Brevet majorities, and so on. Of course such things are possible. For my own part I shall (God helping me) do my duty without sparing myself, but besides the fact of my having had no experience of the field, not even as many have of 'Autumn Manoeuvres',[3] I do not believe I am naturally fitted for action of any brilliant kind in field service. I therefore do not expect or aspire to a Brevet, though, of course, I should be glad to be so successful, chiefly for my father's sake, as I know it would please him. I hope, however, that Arthur will get his Brevet for Afghanistan.'

Medals, Brevet-ranks, Mentions in Despatches – these were the forms of recognition from above that British officers sought on active service. Few officers had seen combat since the major campaigns of the 1850s – the Crimea and the mutiny of the Bengal army. There had of course been a good number of very minor colonial operations in India, China, New Zealand and Canada, as well as African expeditions against the kings Theodore of Abyssinia (1868) and Kofi of Ashanti (1873–4). None of these campaigns was large enough to employ more than a handful of officers, and more often than not it was the Indian Army establishment – the British and Indian units stationed in the sub-continent – that was called upon for duty. Modern readers tend to associate the 'High Victorian' era with a dense succession of significant wars in Egypt, the Sudan and South Africa. However – if we leave aside the scrappy and small-scale bush campaigns of the Eastern Cape – we can see that it was the Afghan and Zulu wars, that were brewing together in the late 1870s, that were actually the first in this string of important 'Small Wars'. Before 1879 there were few in the Home Army, at least, who had very much idea of actual service conditions.

The 'Brevet' was a promotion in the field, which was likely to be formally confirmed at the end of the campaign in question. In the years following the abolition of purchased commissions in 1871, all promotion in the British

Army was otherwise strictly by seniority. With few opportunities for active service, and what appeared to be a disturbingly low mortality rate among their seniors, young regimental officers were anxious to exploit absolutely every means of improving their career chances that they could – including the dangers often attached to promotion by Brevet. As an older, less impressionable family man, by contrast, Warren Wynne was far less attracted to the trappings of martial success. He did nevertheless achieve his Brevet promotion to Major.

Spending Christmas away from Lucy and his three sons was understandably difficult for Wynne:

¶ 'Christmas Day – I began the day by thanking God for that which we commemorate upon it, and then wished for you a 'Happy Christmas' in the truest sense of the words, and prayed that when it comes round next, we may spend it together with the dear children around us. I must say it has been very difficult to realise the fact of its being Christmas Day as far as external appearances go. I can but imagine your Christmas at home, with all the dear ones round you; the joyous church services, the congratulations, the Christmas cards, and above all the happy faces of the children.

We ought to be at Cape Town early on Saturday, ie three days hence, and glad indeed shall I be to be on terra firma again, and to learn particulars as to what is before us. I hope that by giving Cetshwayo and the Zulus a crushing blow now, they may be kept quiet for a long time to come.

I wonder whether the London papers will sent out any correspondent to inform people at home of our doings. I hope so, for I shall find it difficult to communicate with you when in the field. I expect, however, that the Afghan affair will so eclipse ours that but scanty notice will be taken of it, and yet to compare the two foes both as regards numbers and prowess ours is the most formidable by all accounts, in cunning also, but their arms are inferior. I hope I shall hear something of their doings out there before we go up to the front. This time last year Arthur was busy with his signalling operations in the expedition against the Jowakies.[4] I wonder how he has succeeded this year in Afghanistan. I should like to train some signallers for our expedition, and may perhaps do so, for they would be very useful; but with so many other things on hand it is doubtful whether I could manage it.'

Arthur Wynne, presently in winter quarters in the Kurram Valley, was responsible for heliostat operations for Major General Frederick Roberts' column. The heliostat was the immediate precursor to the newer heliograph, just now coming into service. Both devices used mirrors set on a tripod rest, to flash coded signals to distant observers. The difference was that the fixed mirror of the earlier design was replaced by a hinged glass on a pivot.

It is interesting, from the distance of more than a century, to note the assumption that the forthcoming Zulu campaign would be a pretty minor affair compared to the large scale invasion of Afghanistan undertaken by Lord Lytton, Viceroy of India, earlier in the year. We have become accustomed, in looking back at the myths and totems of the Victorian Age, to imagine the Zulu War as the central tableau in a display of glorious martial events ranging from Balaclava to Mafeking. For four generations of Britons, the disaster of Isandhlwana and the heroic defence of Rorke's Drift – along with Jack the Ripper and the introduction of flush toilets – have been part of that fund of common knowledge which passes as 'Victorian History'. From Warren Wynne's viewpoint in December 1878, however, there was nothing to suggest this small and globally insignificant affair on the African frontier would be of any special interest to anyone. It is today worth remembering that – setting aside the Music Hall's interest in dancing Zulus, and the Cinema's in gallant technicolor redcoats – the Zulu War actually was a very unimportant campaign by comparison with the three year struggle to wrench Afghanistan from the clutches of the Czar.

¶ 'Cape Town, December 28th, 7.30am – We arrived at 11.40pm yesterday. This morning the news has come on board that the women and children are to disembark, and perhaps the heavy baggage. Cetshwayo has received an ultimatum which expires in a week, and we are ordered up to the front at once. It is overwhelming to me to think of such a thing as far as the RE is concerned, with all our heaps of stores to sort out, to arrange, and to pack – to say nothing of organising the men, the majority of whom are recruits.

Captain Jones[5] and I landed, and lunched with Major and Mrs Nixon,[6] and afterwards went out by train to Wynberg[7] to pay our respects to Lady Frere, the Governor's wife. She was having a garden party, so we saw something of Cape society. We found the country most beautiful two miles out from Cape Town. Such beautiful green foliage, and the Table Mountain grand; also the distant mountains beautiful in outline and hue. There was a delicious breeze, and for a day in summer nothing could be more perfect. The drawback to the place is the dust, a red sand, which covers one if the

THE PLAN OF CAMPAIGN

Lord Chelmsford's strategy was to invade Zululand by means of several columns converging on Cetshwayo's capital at Ulundi. A number of self-contained forces could avoid the expected delays of moving one large column over the rough tracks and drifts of Zululand, and would be more likely to force the enemy to a decisive battle, for Chelmsford's chief fear was that the highly mobile Zulus would avoid contact with the Red Soldiers, and strike directly into Natal. The campaign was set for January, during the wet season when the River Tugela was high enough to prevent the Zulus from crossing except at the well-guarded drifts. The Zulu maize crops were still in the fields, and grain stocks would be low at the kraals. This plan was open to serious criticism as to the risks of splitting an army in the face of the much larger Zulu army.

The columns were to be arranged as follows:

Column No 1: commanded by Colonel Pearson of the Buffs, comprising 4,750 all ranks, advancing along the road via Eshowe. Captain Wynne's company was attached to the No 1 Column.

Column No 2: under Colonel Durnford, based on Middle Drift as a mobile reserve, according to Chelmsford's orders: 3,871 troops, consisting almost entirely of NNC.

Column No 3: under Colonel Glyn of the 24th, ordered to advance through central Zululand via Rorke's Drift: 4,709 all ranks, accompanied by GOC and staff.

Column No 4: 2,278 officers and men under Sir Evelyn Wood, marching from Utrecht into the disputed Western borderlands of Zululand.

Column No 5: under Colonel Rowlands, advancing from the Northern Transvaal with 1,565 all ranks. (Columns no. 2 and 5 were auxiliary forces, supporting the advance of the stronger forces).

Colonel Charles Knight Pearson (1834–1909) of the 3rd Regiment of Foot – known as 'The Buffs' after the colour of the contrasting trim on their red coats – was a career army man, like most of his peers. Compared with many of the other officers who served in Zululand, Pearson remains an obscure figure. He was a steady regimental officer, dutiful and dependable; but not destined for great things. His orders were to advance from the mouth of of the River Tugela to establish a stores depot at the mission station of Eshowe; then march inland towards Ulundi. His striking force was based upon two battalions of regular infantry – his own 2/3rd Regiment, and Lt Col Welman's 99th. These reliable troops were augmented by detachments of gunners, and mounted infantry and Royal Naval landing parties from HMS *Active*, *Tenedos* and *Shah*. Besides these Imperial contingents, there were units of local colonists serving as mounted volunteers, and two large battalions of the Natal Native Contingent. The NNC consisted of Natal Africans and refugees from Zululand, many of them unwillingly enlisted, and bearing a traditional dread of the Zulu impis. Armaments and dress were rudimentary – a red rag around the head: a firearm for every tenth man, and a bundle of light spears. The junior officers and ncos were recruited from the colony's shifting population of loafers and drifters, and treated their men with a casual brutality. The NNC were expected to work rather than to fight – but nobody really expected much from them at all.

wind be blowing much. It was certainly additionally agreeable to have such a pleasant outing after our long sea voyage.'

¶ 'Sunday, 29th – I went to see the women and children of the Company in the quarters which had been told off to them here in The Castle. They have one very large Barrack room for the six women and five children,[8] and seem pretty satisfied.

I went with the Nixons to the Military Chapel, and was indeed glad to join in the dear old service again. I had intended going to Holy Communion at the Cathedral at 8am, but was prevented by duty on board, and there was not any at the midday service. While I think of it, please tell everybody that I have found it impossible to do more than write this single letter, as there is so much to be done and thought about. Give all my kind love. I will not forget darling Harry[9] on his birthday.

I went with the Nixons to the Cathedral this evening – the service was very nicely conducted. A Happy New Year, and every blessing to all. We leave at 4 pm for Durban, from which place I shall write again.'

While the *Walmer Castle* was steaming towards the Cape, matters had taken a course of their own in South Africa. Sir Bartle Frere, convinced that war with the Zulus was inevitable, had taken steps to ensure that it began at a time of his own choosing. On December 11th the results of the Boundary Commission were presented to Cetshwayo's emissaries. Although the findings of the commission generally favoured the Zulus' land claims, they were followed by a piece of work by Frere which would ensure that there could be no peaceful resolution. The Boers who chose to leave the disputed territory were to receive compensation from the Zulus, and there was to be a British Resident. However the item that made hostilities inevitable was an astonishing ultimatum: the Zulu army was to be dissolved; executions without formal trial were to cease, and Zulu men were to be free to marry as and when they chose. These demands, along with some lesser requirements, were to be met within thirty days. Even now, Cetshwayo made efforts towards conciliation – but it was always evident that compliance was out of the question. If the ultimatum came as a shock to Cetshwayo, it was even more of a surprise to Sir Michael Hicks Beach at the Colonial Office, who knew nothing of it until 2nd January.

Sir Bartle Frere was to have his war after all.

1) This regulation served to ensure that vessels did not sail before regiments had been given a chance to check that all officers, men, animals and stores were actually on board.
2) Captain Arthur Wynne, 51st Regiment of Foot, was appointed as Superintendant of Army Signalling for the Kurram Valley Field Force. He served at the actions of Peiwar Kotal, the Mangior Pass and Matun. He was mentioned in despatches, and was brevetted Major.
3) The annual field exercises for Infantry, Cavalry and Artillery did not provide adequate opportunities to perform their specialist skills.
4) The Jowaki, or Jawaki Afridis, were a Pathan tribal group of the North West Frontier, and had been subject to a British 'punitive expedition' in 1878.
5) Captain Walter Parke Jones entered the Royal Engineers in 1864, received his Captaincy in 1877, and commanded the 5th Field Company throughout the Zulu War. He resigned his commission in November 1879, and died in Paris four years later.
6) Major Francis William Nixon, RE, had passed out of Woolwich two years before Warren Wynne. He commanded the engineers in the field in the 9th Frontier War – but he was left in Cape Town as commandant of the RE depot, in December 1878.
7) The Governor's Residence was at Wynberg – a small town noted for its vineyards.
8) The British Army allowed six soldiers' wives 'on the strength of' each company.
9) Harry was Wynne's second son, and almost two years old at this time.

Chapter Three: Natal – Marching to the Front

¶ 'SS WALMER CASTLE, Durban Harbour, 3rd January, 1879 – We ought to have arrived here at midnight, but the sea was rough and weather thick, so the Captain stood out to sea considerably, and afterwards changed his course, so that we did not arrive till midday to-day, and we are now riding at anchor in the roadstead, earnestly wishing that human ingenuity would overcome the objectionable bar at the mouth of the harbour which prevents large ships from entering. We are waiting for the Staff Officer to come on board, and tell us our instructions. We hear that Cetshwayo has deigned no answer to the ultimatum, and is advancing with troops to meet us; and that our forces are to advance at once, so as to commence operations on the 10th. The Staff Officer has come on board. The 99th are to land at once, and push on to-morrow. We probably go ashore to-morrow, and shall have to wait two or three days while they provide us with mules. I hope to be able to post this at Durban by the mail that leaves to-morrow or next day. Cetshwayo is in great force, and believes himself a match for the troops we can send against him. He is said to be marching troops to the frontier. So much the better for us, for we shall not have so much trouble penetrating the country to search him out. I sincerely hope we may now settle his business quickly, and so settle down at our station all the sooner. It is sure to be a flying column kind of work, and therefore I feel there will be little chance of sending letters; you must not therefore be uncomfortable if you are left without news for some time, though I hope it may not be long.'

Durban[1] was the port for Natal, and the landing place for HM forces en route for the Zulu campaign. It was not much of a port. The mouth of the harbour was blocked to ocean going vessels by a sandbar, which all attempts to remove had failed. Sometimes there was twelve feet of water, sometimes only three, and few captains wanted to risk their keels on the chance of a lucky passage. Instead, ships would wait in the open roadstead while the cargo and passengers were loaded into 'lighters' – small harbour vessels – for the short but uncomfortable last leg of the voyage:

¶ 'DURBAN, 5th January – The first sheet of my letter written on board the *Walmer Castle* is a disgraceful production, and I fear you will be scarcely able to read it. We were up at 4am yesterday, and ready at 5 to disembark from the ship into a small tug, which had to cross the bar of Durban, which is often so troublesome as to make landing here a matter of great difficulty or even impossibility. I got my men an early light meal of tea and bread, and then we had to wait, wait, wait, till about 7.30, when we packed close as dried herrings on board the tug, and found the bar, as we crossed it, propitious. Landed at the Government wharf, and marched up to the Camp about two miles off. There I found that, notwithstanding my having sent careful notice of my requirements on the day before, the commissariat had taken no steps whatever to provide rations for my men, and I had to start off and wander through the town in search of these commissariat people, and then to the butcher, baker, etc., who had the contract, to entreat them to send rations to my men, who had now been long fasting. Then I had to search out the Commissary of Stores in another department to obtain tents, camp kettles etc. etc, and for $2^1/_2$ hours was I walking about searching for this individual; the upshot of all being that it was 2pm before either my men or their officers got a meal, though they had been pretty hardly worked since early morning. Our mode of disembarking from the *Walmer Castle* was peculiar. We were dropped, or I should say slung, and let down by a basket over the side of the vessel down into the tug. The people have been hospitable, and have given us the use of the Club, so we have not yet had to live on camp rations, which I expect will be pretty tough. Last night I spent my first night in a tent. It poured the whole night in torrents, and blew too. The frogs croaked, grasshoppers chirped, and what with the day's excitement and work (for we worked hard all day at our stores besides the pitching of the camp) and these noises, I got but two hours' sleep. To-day we have had continual work. How I shall long for another peaceful Sunday! I succeeded in getting a fine large railway shed, wherein to sort our stores, and we have been shunting trucks and unloading them nearly all day. Courtney and the two other subalterns have worked splendidly.

We are to start if possibly on Tuesday morning for the Tugela, to join Colonel Pearson's Column. There I am to have under my command a Company of

Native Pioneers,[2] in addition to my present Company.

May God give me help to do my duty rightly and successfully, for I feel of myself unequal to it! We go with a train of seven mule waggons, sixty-two mules, and fourteen horses, and some ox-waggons also are to follow if not ready by Tuesday. It will be a heavy responsibility. In a week's time we shall probably have crossed into Zululand. I will write a line or two to-morrow, which is all I shall have time for. It will be the hardest day of all.

Once ashore, things had not improved. The traditional belief that the British army could go to war with no supplies or transport – the approach that had caused so much difficulty in the Crimea a generation before – was in its death throes. Lord Chelmsford's plans made elaborate calculations as to stores, draught animals and wagons required for the expedition; however, the plans demanded adequate numbers of officers skilled in the practical details of organising a campaign, and these the Queen's forces in Natal did not have. Most of the officers of the Commissariat and Ordnance Stores Department were still in transit for South Africa when Wynne arrived at Durban. The skeleton staff present in Natal was forced to make use of local civilians, and the clerical work that was supposed to ensure that troops who landed had somewhere to go and something to eat, simply collapsed. The commissaries worked themselves hard – De Ricci, the responsible man in Durban for most of the war, had to be invalided home from the strain – but, with the stores depot two miles from the landing place at the Point, the harbour jammed with bobbing lighters and fresh troopships lined up in the roadstead, the situation deteriorated rapidly. For a man like Wynne, whose orderly efficiency had not been tempered by the experience of campaign improvisation, the first days in Natal must have been daunting. The brief letters to Lucy show him getting to grips with the untidy realities of it all:

¶ '6th January – Overwhelmed with work and scarcely time even for a farewell. We march to-morrow, and expect to cross the Tugela about the 12th. I am very well, thank God. Best love to all dear ones.'

¶ '7th January – After immense toil and worry, I have succeeded in getting the Company prepared to start this afternoon for the first march towards the Tugela. We are to go with Colonel Pearson's Column, which crosses into Zululand by the river Tugela, near its mouth. We have sixty-six miles to march thither. I take with me, altogether, twenty-six waggons, nineteen horses, fifty-six mules, 316 oxen,[3] and (for food) twenty-eight sheep. The men have behaved very well, and the officers have worked as hard as possible. The stores etc of half a pontoon troop, besides other bridge equipment, follow for me in two or three days.[4] After the survey work, which used to be racketing enough in the way of travelling etc, I find that I came from easy and peaceable compared with this; and, unfortunately, the heavy responsibility works upon me and curtails my needed nights' rest. However, I trust things will work into some shape before we become engaged. I am in capital health, thank God, and only wish I was properly competent for my post. I will write again as soon as there is a chance. I go to Verulam first, then Stanger, then Tugela, then...?'

¶ 'VERULAM, 9th January – The last chance of sending a line for some time. Our first day's march yesterday was a trying one. Torrents of rain, roads fearful, and our mule train stuck in a river four miles behind us, so that late in the evening we were without tents or rations. Fortunately we were able to re-cross a river here, and put up the men in a Volunteer Drill Hall,[5] and I bought up all the provisions I could get, and fed the men well. The mule train arrived about midnight. To-day is fearfully wet, but we must push on. I am pressing in two more ox-waggons, to diminish the loads of the others, and hope to get on without sticking. It is nasty wet work, but we are in good health. I had to carry the rifle of one man, who was faint through marching. The rest did pretty well.'

It was at this time that Warren Wynne began the Diary that he would keep until he fell victim to the fever that was to kill him. He began with a cursory notation of the voyage to Natal. This was followed by brief comments on the first days of the campaign, in the clipped, accurate style that was to distinguish the Diary entries:

¶ 'January 4th to 7th. – Occupied in landing and sorting out equipment and stores, a troublesome work, owing to their confusion with those of other Regiments and Departments.'

¶ 'January 7th. – Left Durban with Company and Equipment by rail for Saccarine. Despatched waggon train (7 mule wagon & 1 ox wagon) and 13 horses by road to Saccarine. Road very heavy. Distance 12 miles. Heavy rains immediately after our arrival at Camp Saccarine at 5pm, and all night.'

On the 11th, Wynne had time to write a longer letter to his wife. The column had reached the township of Stanger, a bustling metropolis by the standards

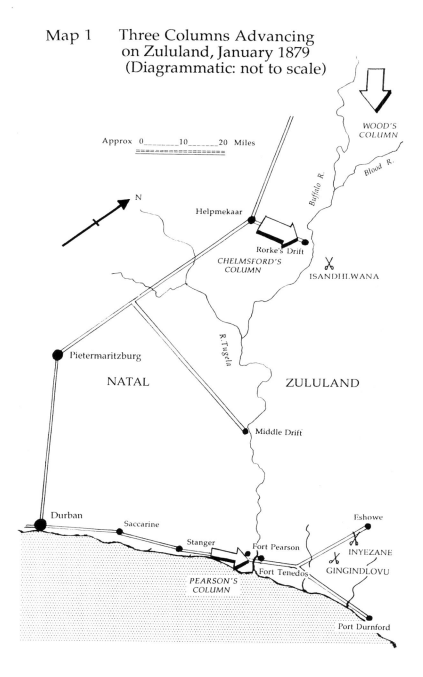

Map 1   Three Columns Advancing
         on Zululand, January 1879
         (Diagrammatic: not to scale)

WOOD'S
COLUMN

Buffalo R.

Blood R.

Approx 0_____10_____20 Miles

N

Helpmekaar

Rorke's Drift

CHELMSFORD'S
COLUMN

ISANDHLWANA

R.Tugela

Pietermaritzburg

NATAL

ZULULAND

Middle Drift

Durban

Saccarine

Eshowe

Stanger

Fort Pearson

INYEZANE

Fort Tenedos

GINGINDLOVU

PEARSON'S
COLUMN

Port Durnford

of frontier Natal. From here Captain Wynne was able to consider the progress made since his company marched out of Durban.

¶ 'STANGER, 11th January – I have but little spare time to write, but must endeavour to send a letter before the active work begins. I will give you a short account of our march so far. On the 7th January we left Durban, as I have already told you, in three detachments, ie a party with camp equipage by 9.30 train, a party with Company equipment (tools and stores of various kinds) at 1pm, and the remainder of the Company with the Officers by the 3.35 train for Saccharine, twelve miles from Durban. The horse and empty mule and ox waggons were sent on by road to the same place, because the road was so heavy with deep sand. I arrived at Saccharine with the Company at 5pm, and we found tents pitched, ready for us, by the party sent in the morning. We had scarcely arrived when the rain fell in torrents, and continued all night and next day.'

¶ '8th January – I wanted to load our mule waggon train in a systematic way, but the cantankerousness of the mules and one thing or another prevented my fully accomplishing it as I wished. I found it very difficult with the inertness of the native drivers, and the want of energy of the white conductor, to get any sort of progress.

My men were on 'fatigue' all the morning, and up to 3pm very wet, and thus had to march off at 3.30 or a camping ground beyond the Umhloti River seven miles off. We started, and I left Courtney with a party of mounted men to bring the waggon train, which, besides the equipment, contained our tents, baggage, and provisions, on to the proposed camping ground.

Meanwhile the heavy rain fell, and the first river to be crossed, the Umhlanga, I found to have risen to 20 inches at the ford. There was a railway bridge over the river in the course of construction, and I made use of it to get the men across dryshod.

We then went on through Verulam, six miles to the Umhloti River, which we forded, depth 18 inches, and I looked out a camping ground. This had no sooner been done than intelligence reached us that the waggons, carrying tents and provisions, had stuck fast in the Umhlanga Ford, and some of the mule waggons at a place further back, and that they could not arrive till long after dark. In my dilemma I was kindly offered, and accepted, accommodation for my men in the Volunteer Drill Hall of Verulam, so at

7pm we re-crossed the Umhloti and marched to the Hall at Verulam. I bought bread, tea, etc., for the men, and a small quantity of spirits to be served to each, and they made themselves comfortable. Courtney, Willock, and I went to the hotel, which was very clean and satisfactory. Haynes, my junior subaltern, I had to leave at Durban to bring on the pontoons. The waggons did not turn up at Verulam till 1am next morning.'

The Diary entry for the 8th was longer than the first few pieces. It consisted of the same basic facts as those in the letter to Lucy; the style, however, is notably different, and there are minor variations in matters of detail. A soldier in the field might, after all, forget the depth of a stream or the precise moment that a march began.

¶ 'January 8th – Heavy rains all the morning. Loaded waggons with stores and equipment from railway trucks. Found transport insufficient, mules untrained and rather unmanageable, delays in consequence. Could not leave Saccharine before 3pm. Left Courtney and some mounted men to escort wagons.

Company marched off at about 3pm, crossed Umhlanga, greatest depth 16'. Reached Verulam at 5.30pm and crossed Umhloti, which lies below (depth 18") and halted near proposed camp, just the other side. Soon after, intelligence received that the wagons had stuck fast in the Umhlanga and could not be up till after dark.

Recrossed Umhloti and procured quarters for the men in the volunteer drill hall at Verulam.

Purchased provisions there for an evening meal for the men, also gave a small quantity of spirits to each on account of their wetting.

The waggons did not arrive till 1am.'

It was fortunate that Wynne and his officers found cheerful lodgings after a wet day of marching, for the following morning was to bring more of the same; the constant rain of the Natal wet season served to mush the ill-defined 'road' into a quagmire as men, animals and wagons tramped over its surface. Once again the captain was to show initiative in assuring that his command benefitted from some of the small comforts of life on campaign – dry feet, a part-way decent billet and a meal of extremely fresh mutton. And, once again, the transport was delayed.

¶ '9th January – Reveillé at 5am; very wet. I seized upon an empty ox waggon going to Tugela[6] and used it to lighten the loads of my others. We were not able to get away from Verulam till 9am. The Umhloti Ford was much deeper than last night, but I fortunately got the loan of an empty waggon to take the men across, 10 at a time. Width of river, 90 yards. The first of our ox waggons stuck in the river through the breaking of some of the gear of the span of oxen. Had to send another span (16 animals) to help them over.

The last of the men were across by 11am. I marched off with the Company at 11, leaving C. and mounted men to bring on the waggon train. The weather was better, but still showery. We ascended a long steep hill; halted at 11.40 for half-an-hour, then traversed a long plateau. At 12.25 descended by a gentle slope to a pretty valley dotted with a variety of handsome shrubs in clumps, Palmettos, Cacti, Aloes, etc., and beautiful bright-coloured wild flowers. The road, however, was frightfully bad. The surrounding country very pretty, undulating, and park-like. At 1pm halted 15 minutes – road very bad – reached Victoria at 2. After waiting a long while, a mounted orderly arrived to say that it was doubtful when the waggons could be up. In order to make quite sure, I procured a rather dilapidated schoolroom and two outhouses for the men, and a sort of storeroom for the officers, through the roof of which one could see the sky and feel the rain, about the walls of which crawled a variety of insects. Our waggons turned up at 6.30pm. Meanwhile our men got their dinners pretty comfortably, the sheep which march with us, being slaughtered, poor things, immediately they are required.

Wynne's Diary entry for the same day adds some of the details of these proceedings:

¶ 'Chartered an empty ox waggon on its way to the Tugela in order to furnish more sufficient transport for our stores. Re-adjusted the loads and left 15 boxes of ammunition in charge of the resident magistrate. Reported to Commandant. Left Verulam at 9am with company and train. Heavy rain. Umhloti Ford 22' deep. Empty waggons passing to front having been placed at my service, the dismounted men were carried over dryshod. Company all across Umhloti Ford by 11am, ten taken at a time. As to the waggon trains, the first ox waggon stuck about three-fourths across the ford, helped it out

TRANSPORT

The invasion orders demanded a solid basis in transport vehicles and draught animals. Prior to the opening of the campaign, Chelmsford's agents purchased or hired 977 wagons, 56 carts, 10,023 oxen, 803 horses and 398 mules, from all over South Africa and beyond; 90% of all the wagons and teams in Natal were employed in Government service. Of these, about $1/3$ were assigned to No 1 Column. The characteristic wagon of Southern Africa was developed by the frontier Boers; it was long and narrow, with a canvas cover, and looked much like the American Conestoga wagon of the western settlers. Fully laden, the wagon might carry 8,000 lbs over a good road. There were, however, hardly any good roads, and it was a foolish man who expected to move a wagon across the veldt with more than 2 – 3,000 lbs aboard; even then, break downs were common. 'Spans' of 16 oxen, in eight pairs, were standard, and doubled teams were required for deep river crossings or steep hills. Oxen were relatively cheap and needed no forage other than the grass on the ground, but demanded careful attention and frequent halts for rest and grazing. In the hands of the inexperienced British soldiers, or hired conductors and 'Voorloopers' (drivers) who cared little for their charges, the oxen were driven too hard and too long. Foul weather, sickness and overwork killed hundreds of animals. No 1 Column was short of oxen from the first, with 8 – 9 per wagon, teams so small that they could barely move over the rough terrain at all. The alternative to ox transport was to use teams of 8 mules, which could double the 8 – 10 miles per day that an ox-wagon could manage, and had the sense to refuse further efforts rather than drop dead in their traces. Mules, however, were ill-tempered, in short supply and - most important of all - each required 120 lbs of forage per day. Wynne's engineers carried vital equipment that would be needed at the front of the advance, and so got priority for the more mobile mule wagons - a privilege the Captain probably did not fully appreciate as he dealt with the pleasures of handling the temperamental beasts for the first time.

by a double span. The 2nd ox and 4 mule waggons across by 11am.'

Interestingly enough, the road he had described to Lucy as 'frightfully bad' was listed curtly in the Diary as 'fair'; perhaps the standards accepted by a soldier on service in South Africa seemed rather different to those which Wynne thought his wife would recognise. However, since he also recorded that the company had reached Victoria at 3.30 rather than 2pm as stated in the letter, it is possible that he simply made a mistake. In both accounts the wagons finally arrived at 6.30pm, for which small mercy we can be sure Wynne was grateful. A commanding officer could not expect any rest until his whole force was accounted for, and he was planning another early reveillé for the morrow:

¶ '10th January – Up at 4am; fine day. Paraded for march at 5.45. Crossed Tongaati River at 7.15 to 7.45. Empty waggons luckily passing, I got the men across dry. We marched $4^1/_2$ miles along an ankle-deep road, and then came to some pasturage land and halted on a slope at 9.30, waiting for our waggons and provisions. Meanwhile the cooks prepared field kitchens, and procured wood and water. At 10.30 the waggon came up; at 12.30 we dined.

At 1.30 marched off, found the road rather better. Obtained fine views of the mountain range, Great Noodbsberg. Came to Umhlati River at 4.45, got the men's arms and clothes taken over, and made them go over for the most part stripped to give them the opportunity of a bathe. The air was delicious. It has never been hotter than a pleasant English summer's day. The shrubs and wild flowers are very striking; Cacti grow 20 feet high.

We marched $1^1/_2$ miles beyond the Umhlati to a high ground, where we waited to encamp. It was dark at 8pm, before the provisions and the tents arrived, and we had to pitch camp in the dark. When we had with difficulty done so, the full moon arose in splendour. The tents, which had not been unpacked since their drenching and 'bemuddying' at Saccharine, were not pleasant.

I got my first wound to-day, and it does not sound well when I say that I got it 'cutting my stick'. I was getting a switch for my horse, when the knife slipped and cut a slice very nearly an inch long off my little finger. I had it quickly tied up in rag.

My health, thank God, is very good indeed. Our food is not very varied. Sheep and indifferent biscuit and moderate tea and coffee day after day, with water as one finds it.'

Wynne's diary entry for the day was light on fresh air and wild flowers, but heavy on the kind of military specifics that a keen Woolwich man might concern himself with. Topography was a key subject for an officer of engineers; and the tight-lipped style of Wynne's description would be immediately familiar to anyone holding a Queen's Commission. Special concern is – very properly – expressed about the condition of the water supply at halting places, for it was accepted that many more British soldiers would die of disease than from enemy action.

¶ 'Crossed Tongaati between 7.15am and 7.45am. Slight ascent in road thence. Road for half-a-mile from Tongaati good, then half-a-mile fair. Good camping ground to the right at one mile from Tongaati; ascended ridge, (skirted by a tributary of the Tongaati) and traversed it. Road bad, at 8.20 halted ten minutes. Country wooded, hill sides steep. At 9.15 descended into a flat and up a gentle slope to about threequarters of a mile from Compensation Flats. There we halted for mid-day meal. Water fair.
Distances - Verulam to Umvoti, said to be – 17 miles

'Stanger, – 21$^1/_2$'
'Tongaati to Compensation Flats – 5'
'Williamstown – 6'
'Umhlati – 9'

Dined at 12.30pm. Marched off at 1.30pm by Compensation Flats. Flats well drained in parts, water fair; half-a-mile from Flats, a very swampy piece of ground. Fair bridges across small streams. At 3.20 passed Williamstown, three-quarters mile to the right. At 4.45pm crossed Umhlati, men bathed, left at 5.10pm, road for 1$^1/_2$ miles bad; at three-quarter mile from the Umhlati rather steep ascent. Halted for night on hill side, 1 $^1/_2$ miles from Umhlati, eleven miles from Victoria; water good and sufficient in water course below. Ox waggon stuck fast in swamps near Compensation Flats, had to be unloaded. Waggons arrived at 8pm, tents pitched in the dark, evening meal at 9, fine weather all day. Courtney, as usual, performed good service in bringing on the waggons.'

In a march of twelve hours, the company had crossed two rivers, advanced eleven miles, and seized the chance for a dip in a stream. Despite apparently easy passage of the drifts, the wagons were late once again. To a soldier accustomed to the leisurely movement of troops along the well-kept highways of England, the sheer difficulty of movement in this primitive land must have seemed daunting. Some thirty miles away, Wynne's friend and fellow engineer, Captain Walter Parke Jones, was writing: 'It has rained in torrents for the last two days, clean through our tents and all one's worldly goods are very damp...' The men knew little of these kind of duties, Jones frankly stating that his sappers 'have no more idea of packing a waggon, kneehaltering a horse or anything of that sort...' All over Natal untrained transport officers were working ox teams to death, losing wagons in swollen rivers, purchasing sick animals as replacements, and taking the stick to uncomprehending Bantu Voorloopers. Rankers went without rations that had been lost en route, or ate strange berries that upset their stomachs. Wynne was therefore coping well, since he had not lost a single animal, yet.

¶ '11th January – Up at 6, gave the men time to get well cleaned, for they have been getting covered with mud from head to foot. An ox wagon broke down yesterday and upset in a quagmire, and having been unloaded, had to be dug out. The same stuck fast last night in the Umhlati. We had to send down this morning to get it out. We marched off at 10.45am; arrived at Umvoti River at 1pm. Water up to the waist, width 100 yards. Began to prepare for dinners. A thunderstorm came on, so I determined to push on four miles to Stanger. I rode on to look for a camp, and the Company arrived at 3.30pm.

This is the depot for the Tugela Column. We hear the first shots were fired this morning. I have determined to push on to-morrow, though whether I shall get the waggons through 17 miles of bad road, with two rivers and promise of bad weather, is doubtful. I have sent on the tents to-night, and have put up the men in a shed. We (officers) are in a place which calls itself 'hotel', full of a variety of people.'

Once again the Journal entry fills in the details. The first mention of sickness among the transport animals, within a few days of beginning the march, shows something of the delicate nature of the apparently robust trek-oxen. In contrast with the hardy mules, which had a wilful sense of their own mortality, the ox would toil uncomplainingly until he fell dead, often to the very great surprise of his British master; they died in droves:

¶ 'One ox fell down through sickness at starting. At $1^1/_2$ miles a deep stream crosses road, avoided by turning off to the left and coming upon a new piece being constructed with a bridge, then ascended ridge beyond which lies the Umvoti river. Crossed Umvoti ford, placing rifles, trousers, boots and accoutrements in a punt which plies backwards and forwards. Depth to waist. Men waded over by 1.30. Bathed and prepared for dinner, but threatening thunderstorm determined us to push on to Stanger. One ox waggon stuck in Umvoti twenty minutes. Arrived in Stanger 3.30. Occupied a galvanized iron store which Hime,[7] of ours, was erecting for Commissariat. Very wet night. Officers slept at Stanger Hotel.'

¶ 'January 12th – Stanger. Reveille at 4am. Marched off at 6.45. Crossed small stream half-a-mile from Stanger, depth 15'. Halted 8am opposite to sugar mill and large kraal. Road good but clayey and slippery in wet. Ugulen $4^1/_2$ miles at 8.45, at 9 a short halt to fill water-bottles, 10.15 crossed Nonoti ford, a very picturesque spot, river 15 yards, depth 16', rocky bottom, banks wooded, a good deal of bush on south side. Halted here; we all bathed (except Courtney, who was seedy) and the men washed their clothes. Dined at 12.30. Marched off at 2. Halted at Sinkwazi river at 3.10 for fifteen minutes. I left company under Courtney and rode to the front to Fort Pearson on the Tugela to learn where we were to go. The RA and Buffs had crossed that day. The Volunteers, Native Pioneers, and Native Contingent were crossing in the afternoon, and some of the 99th were just about to go over in the punt[8] when I arrived. The punt, a large flat bottomed vessel, about 30 feet long by 11 feet broad, hauled across by natives at either bank by means of a steel hawser, rope and tackle.

¶ I arrived at Tugela at 4.30, reported myself to Colonel Walker,[9] AAG of (Col. Pearson's) No 1 Column. Found Main[10] at Fort Pearson. We were ordered to encamp near Fort Pearson for the night and cross over to Zululand next day.'

NOTES

1) Durban was named after Sir Benjamin D'Urban, who had been a general under Wellington in the Peninsular War, and was later Governor of Cape Colony.
2) The Natal Pioneers were the best element of the NNC. Colonel Durnford had raised three companies, each of 90 men. They wore cast-off red coats of British regulars, carried pickaxes and shovels along with their weapons, and served with distinction.
3) Comprising, one assumes, the 7 mule wagons with 8 draught animals apiece, and 19 trek-wagons pulled by the full spans of 16 oxen each.
4) The equipment did not arrive in time for the opening of the campaign.
5) Volunteer units abounded in South Africa in 1879. Natal had 11 separate mounted corps – amounting to 430 all ranks – 3 infantry companies (272) and the 51 gunners of the Durban Volunteer Artillery.
6) No 3 Column crossed the Tugela at Rorke's Drift early on the morning of January 11th, while Evelyn Wood's No 4 Column advanced into north west Zululand.
7) Captain A H Hine was the Colonial Engineer in Natal. He was appointed commander of the Natal Native Pioneers.
8) The 'punt', or pont, could carry a company of infantry or a laden wagon. It was drawn across the river by a hawser connected to an anchor from *HMS Tenedos*. At first it was powered by African labourers, and later by ox teams. The first casualty of the war was a sailor named Martin who fell into the river from the punt and was killed by a crocodile.
9) Colonel F W E F Walker, Scots Guards (1844 – 1910) had until recently been Military Secretary to Sir Bartle Frere.
10) Lt T R Main RE had served in the Gaika and Gcaleka wars of the Eastern Cape (1877 – 8) and in the Transkei as engineer to Colonel Glyn's command.

Chapter Four: Fort Tenedos – Practical Engineering

Warren Wynne was in his element. Almost seventeen years after being gazetted to a lieutenancy in the Royal Engineers, he was about to use the professional skills that he had learned at the Royal Military Academy. The 1860s and '70s had witnessed a series of wars in Europe and America where the precise sciences of the military engineer – field fortification, signals and mapping – had made great strides forward. Engineers had designed the massive works at Petersburg and Plevna; and the massive power of modern breechloaders – with the resulting emphasis on well-planned defensive works – meant a new lease of life for the arts of fortress-building and siegecraft. This was not something that could easily be practised in peacetime manoeuvres or field days; and the active service offered by the 'small wars' of the Victorian era usually demanded skills of a far more basic nature. There were, after all, few railway mortars or heavy Krupp cannon among the tribes of the Afghan frontier or the Xhosa herdsmen of the Eastern Cape. Wynne was to build a fort. It would not be a fort to hold back brigades of French Zouaves, or withstand the Kaiser's steel breech-loaders: but it would be more than Cetshwayo's Amabutho ever thought to conquer.

¶ 'LOWER TUGELA CAMP, 17th January, 1879 – I think I sent off my last from Stanger. We left it early next morning, and made a good march of $18^1/_2$ miles, on a hot day, to the Tugela. Four men fell out, and had to be carried on the waggons. When we got within four miles of this place I rode on, and reported the approach of my Company. I found that the Buffs, the Native Pioneers, Native Contingent, and RA, had crossed the river, and part of the 99th Regiment were then (4.30pm) in the act of crossing.

We encamped for the night near Fort Pearson, on the Natal side, and were joined by Main, of ours, who has been employed here for some little time.

We crossed over at 2pm next day by the 'Pont', a long flat-bottomed ferry, worked along a hawser which is stretched from shore to shore. The distance is about 280 yards. In the early morning (5am) Colonel Pearson, who commands the column, sent for me to come over. I crossed over and called upon him, and received his instructions and suggestions as to the advisability of establishing a depot for stores and provisions on this side of the water, instead of being dependent on the state of the river, the Pont, etc.

I decidedly concurred in the scheme, and promised to prepare a design at once for a site for a store, and a small fort to surround and protect it (afterwards called Fort Tenedos), with a garrison of about 200 men or more, who would also be employed in loading the waggons going forward with supplies for the column in its advance.

Next morning, before breakfast, I showed him my design, and went on the ground with him. He approved it, and in two or three hours we were at work. We have had large working parties on it, but we came upon rocky ground in excavating the ditch, and it made the progress slow, so that it will not be quite completed when we leave to-morrow. However, the men who will be left behind will not be long finishing it. It has been hard work for my two subalterns, Main and Willock, who have had to be on it superintending from 5am to 7pm, with the exception of an hour for breakfast and the same for dinner. We all have very hard work. Turn out every morning at 3am, under arms, and occupy our alarm posts. Turn in again for a short time till reveillé, which is at 4.30am; after which there is work, work, work till 8pm, when we have to put out our lights, and turn in with our clothes on, ready to turn out again at the sound of the 'Alarm'.

Sometimes I get rather tired of it, but I am, thank God, in capital health, and rest and quiet will be all the more acceptable afterwards. We have had beautiful weather.'

There were already two forts along the lower Tugela. Fort Williamson had been begun in 1861, but had been abandoned since 1870. Instead of rebuilding it, as initially planned, two companies of the Buffs constructed another work on ground overlooking the lower drift. It was named 'Fort Pearson' in honour of the regiment's commander, and consisted of a small hilltop redoubt with a ditch and parapet following the contour line further down the slope. It was a very simple entrenchment, some fifty yards by thirty, and appeared more like a minor Celtic hill fort than the product of modern engineering science. Wynne's project was to build a counterpart to Fort Pearson on the north bank, 600 yards north of the river – for easier distribution of stores. He walked over the ground, tracing the shape of the fort according to the lay of the land. It was to be named after *HMS Tenedos*, which provided a contingent to the Naval Brigade.

Map 2 - The Lower Tugela Theatre
(Diagrammatic: not to scale)

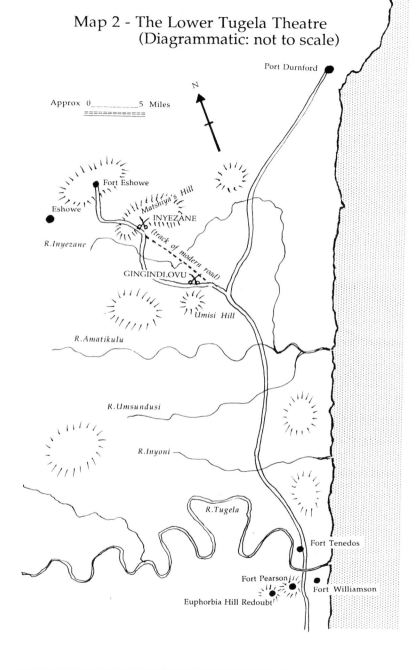

Port Durnford

N

Approx 0 _____ 5 Miles

Fort Eshowe

Matshiya's Hill

Eshowe

INYEZANE

R.Inyezane

(track of modern road)

GINGINDLOVU

Umisi Hill

R.Amatikulu

R.Umsundusi

R.Inyoni

R.Tugela

Fort Tenedos

Fort Pearson

Euphorbia Hill Redoubt

Fort Williamson

¶ 'January 13th – Fort Pearson Camp, Reveillé at 4.30am, at 5.30am message from Colonel Pearson to cross over and see him. Received his instructions with reference to the intention of erecting a provision store, on that side of the river, which would require to be placed within a work defended by a small garrison.

I report that the 'drivers' of my Company were still unarmed, though I had applied for revolvers or any other firearms for them at Durban. Colonel Pearson said that the arms of six invalids[1] of the Buffs might be handed over to me if there were no regimental objection. Wet morning; Company crossed over to camp on opposite bank at 2pm.

Left Corporal Orchard, Sappers Cooksey and Crockett behind for repairs to punt and to look after reserve depot of stores, afterwards, on 18th, left, in addition, Sergeant Campbell, Sappers Besswarick and Church to put up store at Fort Tugela.'

Fort Tenedos was an earthen redoubt, with eight faces of different lengths like a flattened hexagon, and a battery extending towards the north-east. The entrance looked down onto the river, designed with a dog-leg parapet to ensure that an enemy trying to force the gate received fire from three sides. There were to be gun positions at two of the six angles – those facing the north east. The fort was roughly 250 feet by 110. Wynne made a careful record of the construction of Tenedos, detailing the actions of all the men at work on the fort.

¶ 'Construction of Field Fort 'Tenedos' on left bank of Lower Tugela Drift to protect a storehouse, 60' x 50', as a depot for feeding the Column No. 1 in Zulu Expedition.'

¶ 'January 14th – Reveillé 4.30am. Inspected ground for site of fort and made a sketch, survey. Decided upon trace of work.'

Following Wynne's survey, the construction began. Work was divided into three-hour periods known as Reliefs, with specific tasks allotted to each relief according to the point of progress reached. The first step was to break ground, dig out the ditch and so produce the soil for the ramparts. It was a better policy to begin with small parties working on each face, and planning to join at the angles, rather than attempting a mammoth development at one point. Thus, on the afternoon of the 15th, parties of men gathered around the

The science of fortification was a complex discipline with a body of laws and principles, largely impenetrable to the casual observer. Since the advent of gunpowder rendered the medieval castle obsolete, military engineers had developed fortress systems based on low, angular works of earth and stone. They were mathematically precise in layout, infinitely subtle in the problems they posed to a besieger – and wildly expensive to national exchequers. These geometric gems had dominated European warfare in the seventeenth and eighteenth centuries. The figure of the great French master – Sebastien Le Prestre de Vauban (1633–1707) – stood like a colossus astride the world of the military engineer.

His influence extended far beyond the bastions and ravelins of Briançon and Neuf-Brisach, through the nineteenth century – until in 1860 the supremely 'modern' Prussian army relied on Vauban's writings as primary materials for siegecraft. Then a keen, studious captain, tracing out minor earthworks in Zululand, followed in the same tradition. Yet the nineteenth century, with its increasingly powerful new artillery, meant that fortresses built on the classical model were to prove vulnerable in a way that simple, quickly-built works were not. At Belfort in the Franco-Prussian War, two earthern redoubts had withstood massive punishment while Vauban's beautiful masonry fortifications had shattered quickly under German gunfire. At Plevna in 1877 a Turkish garrison, firing breech-loading rifles and showing an astonishing capacity for digging for victory, fended off a Czarist army until starved into submission after 143 days.

Current theories of permanent fortifications were starting to stress works built almost entirely underground, with huge guns that disappeared from sight to reload. The Belgian engineer Brialmont would be spending prodigious sums to safeguard his country's borders in the 1880s – an investment that would prove wasted in face of the Kaiser's guns in 1914. Others were devising their own schemes: Cambrelin's all-iron fortresses; Gruson's armoured gun cupolas; and Mougin's concrete bunkers. For a military engineer, it was a very interesting time!

perimeter of the intended earthwork:

¶ 'January 15th – 1st Relief – 3 to 6pm. RE – 12 Sappers digging sods for revetments; 8 superintending infantry; 5 preparing wood for profile; 6 setting up profiles. Total, 31.

Infantry – 145 Diggers.

Tasks – 5' x 5' x 2'. Fairly well got out. Some sandy soil and light mould; some stiffish clay.'

The 'profile' was a cross-section of the fort. An engineer had to ensure that his completed works were constructed at the correct angles and elevations to assure comprehensive fields of fire, and adequate protection from enemy fire and assault. A more basic problem was that a two-steep rampart would fall down, while one that was too shallow would pose no obstacle to an attacker. The shapes of the profile were laid out using wooden stakes of the correct length, hammered into the ground and often linked by cords or tapes to delineate the required angles. The workmen would then build up to the lines of the profiles. The network of posts and cords was delicate, and the frequent 'alarms' at Eshowe meant that the profiles would require constant repair.

The job assigned to each of the work details – the job of digging out 50 cubic feet of earth – was, according to the manuals, a task that would take some five hours. January being a summer month in the southern hemisphere, there was time enough for five reliefs on the 16th – fifteen hours – which Wynne and his officers supervised throughout. He divided his crews into 'diggers' – those who excavated the ditch – and 'shovellers' who built up the rampart with fresh earth.

¶ 'January 16th – 2nd Relief – 5 to 8am: RE – 1 NCO and 3 sappers preparing wood for profiles; 6 profiling; 1 NCO and 13 superintending. Total, 24. Infantry – 2 cutting drains; 166 diggers; 10 shovellers; 4 preparing wood for drains. Total, 182. 40 infantry did not come till 6am.'

¶ 'January 16th – 3rd Relief – 9 to 12 Noon. RE – 1 NCO and 12 sappers superintending; 3 cutting wood for drains; 4 profiling. Total, 20.

Map 3 - Fort Tenedos

Approx 0_____50 Yards

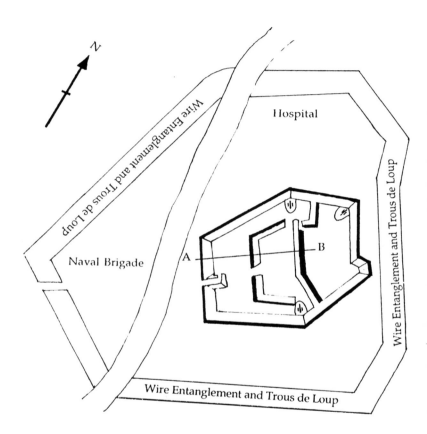

Work done by infantry on different faces at Fort Tenedos

Face A	Diggers	Shovellers	Face D	Diggers	Shovellers
1st Relief	20	–	1st Relief	33	–
2nd Relief	20	3	2nd Relief	33	–
3rd Relief	15	5	3rd Relief	8	2
4th Relief	11	9	4th Relief	12	5
5th Relief	9	1	5th Relief	25	7
6th Relief	27	6	6th Relief	18	3
7th Relief	–	7	7th Relief	–	–
Total	102	31		129	17

Face B	Diggers	Shovellers	Face E	Diggers	Shovellers
1st Relief	32	–	1st Relief	23	–
2nd Relief	34	3	2nd Relief	24	2
3rd Relief	31	7	3rd Relief	20	5
4th Relief	13	7	4th Relief	17	2
5th Relief	13	2	5th Relief	13	1
6th Relief	6	2	6th Relief	–	–
Total	129	21		97	10

Face C (Native Pioneers*)			Face F		
1st Relief	–	–	1st Relief	7	–
2nd Relief	24	–	2nd Relief	–	–
3rd Relief	29	1	3rd Relief	7	3
4th Relief	28	3	4th Relief	5	2
5th Relief	26	3	5th Relief	5	2
6th Relief	21	15	6th Relief	8	4
7th Relief	23	3	7th Relief	1	3
Total	151	29		43	14

Face G			Face H		
1st Relief	3	–	1st Relief	20	–
2nd Relief	1	1	2nd Relief	20	1
3rd Relief	3	–	3rd Relief	17	7
4th Relief	4	1	4th Relief	9	7
5th Relief	5	2	5th Relief	7	3
6th Relief	2	1	6th Relief	21	4
7th Relief	5	5	7th Relief	31	21
Total	23	10		125	43

Total diggers and shovellers – 2,330 and 517 * Face C done exclusively by Native Pioneers.

Revetting, Sod-cutting, etc:

Infantry Work

	Revetting	Getting and wheeling	Drains
Face A	174		)
Face B			)
Face C			)
Face D			) 23
Face E			)
Face FG and gun	46	78	)
Face H	95		)
Total	315	78	23

Hence Grand Total Infantry : 3,253

RE work done

	Superintending	Revetting
Face A	26	68
Face B	30	
Face C	18	
Face D	33	
Face E	27	
Face F, G & gun	36	18
Face H	45	34
Total	215	120

Total 335

Infantry – 130 diggers (28 only 2 hours); 36 shovellers (13 only 2 hours); 18 cutting sods. Total, 184. Of these, 41 did not arrive till 10am.
Tasks in 2nd Relief in some places finished, in others of hard soil not quite.
In 3rd Relief – Tasks, two-thirds done; the soil hard and almost rocky.'

Drainage was an important issue in building a fort, not only for sanitary reasons, but to ensure that water build-up did not damage the works. The simplest way to do this was to dig open trenches for run-off – but Wynne chose underground 'cut and cover' drainage lined with timber, instead.

¶ 'January 16th – 4th Relief – 1 to 4pm. RE – 1 NCO and 15 sappers superintending; 4 profiling; 8 filling and building sand-bags. Total, 28.
Infantry – 99 diggers, 36 shovellers; 18 sod-cutting; 12 sand-bag filling; 12

getting and wheeling earth. Total, 177.
Soil rocky, diggers chiefly finished former incomplete tasks.'

¶ '16th January – 5th Relief – 4 to 7pm. RE – 1 NCO and 4 sappers superintending; 5 building revetments. Total, 10.
Infantry – 103 diggers; 21 shovellers; 2 building in drains; 3 building revetments; 20 filling sand-bags; 18 cutting sods. Total, 177.
Infantry changed three times during this relief, causing much loss of time. Soil very hard.'

The sandbags were used instead of sods for some of the revetments. A drawn plan of Fort Tenedos in the Parliamentary Papers shows an inner defence line of sandbags running between walls A and E, with a ditch of its own. Wynne does not mention this, or a second interior work of gabions, so they were probably of a later construction. Other additions would include three more gun platforms, at angles AB, CD and DE – and an outer barrier of wire entanglements and *trous de loup* surrounding the fort.

¶ 'January 16th – Made a sketch of the ground round the fort. Telegraphed to Haynes by Col. Pearson's orders to bring on only two pontoon rafts complete. Afterwards receiving a telegram from him to say that the pontoons had not arrived by any of the steamers chartered by Government, and could not be at Durban, if at all, before the 25th, by Col. Pearson's order I telegraphed to bid him not wait but come on at once.'

¶ 'January 17th – 6th Relief. – 5 to 8am. RE – 1 NCO and 7 sappers superintending; 5 soil revetting; 2 sand-bag revetting. Total, 15.
Infantry – 103 diggers, 35 shovellers; 15 sand-bags; 8 getting and wheeling. Total, 161.'

¶ 'January 17th – 7th Relief – 9 to 12 (Digger's tasks – 3' x 10' x 1') RE – 1 NCO and 5 sappers superintending; 4 sod revetting; 4 sand-bag revetting. Total, 14.
Infantry – 70 diggers; 43 shovellers; 4 sod revetting; 6 getting and filling. Total, 123.'

By noon on the 17th, Wynne paused to consider the state of progress. The faces that looked towards Zululand were complete, or near to it, but the riverward faces were not. Bowing to pressures of time, Wynne made a note to modify his initial plans.

Map 4 - Fort Tenedos, cross section

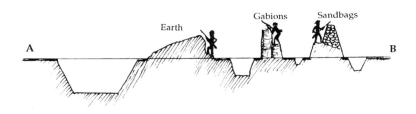

¶ 'GUN PLATFORMS – 1st, in faces f and e; 2nd in angle of faces a and h. At end of 7th relief the faces a, h, g, and f, had been completely revetted, a and gun platform in angle a, h, with sods, remainder with sand-bags. The parapets on faces a and h was on the point of completion, a,^{2} f, and g, $^7/_8$ finished. On the remaining faces revetting had not been begun; but about $^3/_4$ of the earth required had been excavated. In the ditch on face a solid rock was met with, at 4 ft deep, and to complete that face the ditch would have to be widened 6 inches. As the Company, RE, were to leave on the 18th January with Colonel Pearson's leading column it was directed that the Infantry left behind should revet face c, and that a modified form of profile should be adopted for the other faces unfinished.

Received CRE's orders with reference to duties on the line of march and instructions with reference to the putting up of the triple galvanized iron store in the fort, which instructions I afterwards handed over to Sergt Campbell, RE, who was left behind to superintend its erection.

While in camp at Tugela we had to turn out at 3am and stand to arms on our alarm posts; besides this there was one occasion on which the 'alert' sounded in the night, some of the enemy having been visible to one of the picquets.'

Fort Tenedos did not impress all observers. J N Crealock, Chelmsford's military secretary – a man of strong opinions and very little charity – had this to say in February:-

¶ 'It was very lucky the Zulus did not attack this place. Fort Tenedos was originally a house and garden – then a trench around it – now any trace of the house and garden has gone and only a pentagon work with one small flank defence for one front is to be seen. It is completely open to the fire of a long, strong, stony hill 300 yards off!! And no one seemed to know that danger until we arrived!'[3]

Crealock's own record in Zululand, and the low esteem in which he was held by his brother officers, cast doubt on his position as an expert. However, there is no doubt that Wynne built the fort where he was told, rather than where – an an engineer – he might have wished. This was also to be true, a few days later, at Eshowe.

NOTES

1) The term 'invalid' was generally reserved for men whose wounds or sickness precluded imminent recovery to a level where they could resume regimental duties.
2) This seems to be a mistake on the part of the original printer. 'E' would make more sense.
3) Sonia Clarke *Invasion of Zululand* page 140.

Chapter Five: Amatikulu – Incidents on the Road

Fort Tenedos was now complete, so far as Wynne's duties were concerned. The 2nd Field Company was destined for the heart of Zululand. The letter to Lucy, written at Lower Tugela Camp on 17th January, ended with the Captain's assessment of No 1 Column's immediate prospects for the coming march:

¶ 'This column marches to-morrow. A detachment of RE, with the Native Pioneers, heads the column, with Mounted Infantry for escort, so as to make good the roads where necessary. It has just come on to rain, with thunder and lightning, and I fear the roads will be more troublesome than we had hoped.

The remainder of my Company also forms part of the leading column. We are to advance upon Ekowe [Eshowe], which we intend to seize and put in a state of defence, so as to form an advanced depot there.

Our trouble is the having to carry such an enormous quantity of supplies. Our train of ox-waggons will number 150; the troops being 1,300 Infantry, 300 Mounted ditto, 1 Company RE, 2 guns RA, 80 Naval Brigade, 600 Native Contingent, 90 Native Pioneers. The rain is falling in torrents, and the thunder pealing long and loud. Our tent is letting in the water freely, so we shall have a damp start. We always hear plenty of rumours. They say there has been a skirmish with Colonel Glyn's column of an insignificant nature; also that the peace party in Zululand is on the increase. I should be sorry that the question should not be very permanently settled; at the same time, fighting or no fighting, or petty fighting, I shall be glad to have it finished. It is dreadful being so utterly without Sunday services, or anything to remind one (externally at least) of Heavenly things. I have been hoping and longing that I might get a letter before we march up country. However, in a day or two there will be a convoy coming up, so I hope it will bring a letter or two. I wish I could write more, but it is now 'lights out', so I have no chance. We start to-morrow at 3am.'

Of the two rumours that were current at Lower Tugela, the first was true; on January 12th troops from Chelmsford's main column had attacked and

---

NUMBER ONE COLUMN - ORDER OF BATTLE

The *Narrative of the Field Operations Connected with the Zulu War* gives the following order of battle for Colonel Pearson's command:-

No. 1 COLUMN

Colonel Commanding	Colonel Pearson, 3rd Foot
STAFF	
Orderly Officer	Lieutenant Knight, 3rd Foot
Principal Staff Officer	Brevet Colonel Walker, CB, Scots Guards
General Staff Duties	Captain McGregor, 29th Foot
Transport Duties	Captain Pelly Clarke, 103rd Foot
Senior Commissariat Officer	Assistant Commissary Heygat
Sub-District Paymaster	Paymaster Georges
Senior Medical Officer	Surgeon-Major Tarrant
CORPS	
Royal Artillery, two 7 pdrs 11/7 RGA (mule)	Lieutenant Lloyd
Royal Engineers, No 2 Company	Captain Wynne, RE
2nd Battalion 3rd Foo	Brevet Lieutenant-Colonel Parnell, 3rd Foot
99th Foot (6 companies)	Lieutenant-Colonel Welman
Naval Brigade	Commander Campbell, RN
No. 2 Squad, Mounted Infantry	Captain Barrow, 19th Hussars
Natal Hussars	Captain Norton
Durban Mounted Rifles	Captain Shepstone
Alexandra Mounted Rifles	Captain Arbuthnot
Stanger Mounted Rifles	Captain Addison
Victoria Mounted Rifles	Captain Saner
2nd Regiment Natal Native Contingent	Major Graves, 3rd Foot
Staff Officer	Captain Hart, 31st Foot
1st Battalion	Major Graves, 3rd Foot
2nd Battalion	Commandant Nettleton
No. 2 Company Natal Native Pioneer Corps	Captain Beddoes

Wynne's estimate of the total numbers of the column was on the low side; the overall strength amounted to almost 5,000 men, including 312 mounted men, mainly local volunteers, and 2,256 Africans of the NNC. The column had 384 wagons, 3,400 draught oxen, and 620 hired drivers and voorloopers. The artillery component consisted of a pair of 7 pounders and a rocket trough from 11th Battery, 7th Brigade, Royal Garrison Artillery, and two 7 pounders, a Gatling gun and two 24 lb rocket tubes brought in by the Naval Brigade. The RGA rocket trough and one of the Naval tubes do not feature in accounts of the campaign; perhaps they were left at the Tugela forts to bolster the small garrisons.

In view of the poor state of the road, Pearson broke the column into two portions to proceed at intervals one day apart. He would take the leading section of five companies of the Buffs, the Bluejackets, Lloyd's guns, about half the mounted men, and the first battalion NNC; Wynne's command of Engineers and Native Pioneers was to accompany Pearson and attend to the roads and river crossings. Only 50 wagons were allotted to the first 'division'; Welman of the 99th was to bring up a further 80, with the balance left at Lower Tugela Camp, to be sent in a convoy later.

burned the kraal of Sihayo, a paramount Chieftain of the border region. The rise of an influential peace party in Zululand was, however, a pipe dream. Once it became clear that the red soldiers were about to invade their homeland, the voices for submission fell silent. Wynne was probably influenced by those of his comrades who had fought the elusive Xhosa warriors of the Eastern Cape, who preferred to avoid a stand-up fight in favour of raids and ambushes. The Zulus were themselves looking for a fight in the open field.

There had been a change in the transport arrangements for the 2nd Field Company; the increased allowance of wagons was perhaps a reflection of recent experiences that the kind of load that might be safe on a firm, dry highway was likely to mean broken axles and broken timetables along the

---

ROADS AND DRIFTS

Campaigning in South Africa was entirely dependent on the ability of heavily laden Imperial forces to move across a largely roadless country. The *Précis of Information Concerning Zululand*[1] compiled by the Intelligence Department ingenuously claimed that by 'avoiding an occasional mealie field, wagons can travel almost everywhere in Zululand...', a view that the men toiling in the January rain might not have shared. Columns of ox-wagons would turn an earthen road into a quagmire, break down the ramps leading to a drift, and destroy the delicate riverbeds that made the crossings passable. Wynne's work details spent their days filling in bad patches of road with soil, wickerwork hurdles and fascines. Drifts demanded more complex work, a combination of geometric tracing and sweated labour. The Précis featured advice for those venturing forth upon the pathways of Zululand.

'The storms are very sudden, and a small stream is quickly converted into an impassable mountain torrent; during the wet season many of these fords are impassable for weeks together. The time taken... in passing these drifts is often very considerable, and working parties should always be sent on as far ahead as possible to repair them. After every severe storm they will require more or less attention. Big stones should be removed, the sides cut down, and the bottoms filled up; but the more that is done by cutting the sides the better, since the earth put in at the bottom may be washed away in an hour or two, and the drifts once again becomes impassable... when drifts (or hills) are very steep, the wagons should always be double-spanned, that is, two teams of oxen harnessed to them. It is a good plan to halt troops near a drift, so that they may be able to assist with drag ropes if the wagons get into difficulties; but in the case of a stuck wagon it is often quickest to off load at once. It is most important to have more than one drift – several if possible – made across a stream, so that the break down of a single wagon shall not block the whole convoy.'

Reference:

1) An edition of the Précis, 'corrected to January 1879', was available to the officers of Chelmsford's army. A third edition was published for a wider public in 1885, featuring notes from officers who had served in the Zulu War

churning morass that was John Dunn's road. It was, however, the best road in Zululand.

¶ 'January 17th – Packed our waggons, viz: – 5 ox waggons and 4 mule waggons, of which 2 ox waggons were to accompany leading column and the remainder the 2nd column. Total weight carried about 25,500 lbs.'

¶ 'January 18th – Column marched off at 5.30am preceded by advanced guard and Native Pioneers, at 4am. Rain all night, morning misty. Halt at 6.20 for twenty minutes. Undulating grassy hills and easy slopes. At three-quarters of a mile and also at $1^3/_4$ miles swampy places, repaired by Native Pioneers. Halted at 7.50am for breakfast, half-a-mile beyond St. Andrew's Mission Station, misty. Marched off at 11am. Crossed Inyoni stream at 1.30. Encamped 200 yards beyond Inyoni.

Rain commenced at 3pm and poured in torrents all night. Camp on long wet grass.'

The seven miles to the Inyoni ran through open, rolling country that the Intelligence Department reports cosily likened to the Sussex Downs – though the hills were intersected with ravines which might, but fortunately did not, conceal Zulus. The drift was a bad one, narrow and rocky, but by this time Wynne was getting used to the perils of the road.

During the night there was a 'scare', the kind of sudden alarm that, at the least, spoiled a man's sleep, and might bring panic and confusion. The Zulu War witnessed several embarrassing incidents where the imagination of green troops turned a possible sighting into a sudden onslaught of warriors, to be faced with Martini-Henry volleys and artillery fire. One particularly absurd episode, on June 6th, involved several thousand rounds of ammunition loosed off in the direction of the camp picquets, and gave the name 'Fort Funk' to the scene of the crime. In January, however, the British soldier had not had a chance to become afraid of creeping Zulus. That would come soon.

¶ 'January 19th – At 1am the alarm sounded and all turned out and stood to arms at alarm post. A few of the enemy's scouts had been seen. After waiting some time in the rain, dark as pitch, we turned in. At 3am again to arms at alarm post. Reveillé at 4.30am. Marched at 1.45pm for Umsundusi, weather wet, reached Umsundusi at 2.45pm. Drift 65' long, deepest part half-way up a man's thigh.[1] The leading Column and waggons were $3^1/_2$ hours in crossing. We encamped 300 yards beyond river. The 2nd Column left Tugela this morning and arrived at Umsundusi just as we had crossed it. We encamped together. The Umsundusi drift good. Approaches too steep, necessary to use double span of oxen to every waggon. Much bush[2] in parts of road near Umsundusi.

Captain Barrow,[3] commanding mounted infantry, brought in a report of the impassable state of the Amatikulu through floods both for waggons and men. I was sent for by Colonel Pearson. A portion of the ford was said to be $4^1/_2$ feet deep for a width of twenty yards or more, depth diminishing for ten yards on either side, sandy bottom to drift approach on south side partially under water and very stony for twenty yards, south bank thickly covered with mealie gardens[4] and reeds. It was reported that there was higher up a narrower spot where the depth seemed less, but the bottom was rocky and the stream rapid. The approaches also encumbered with boulders. I proposed, if necessary, to form a bridge over present drift by means of crib piers with timber and stones and road bearers of the straightest trees we could get corduroyed over[5] and filled in with brushwood, or to get piers by means of waggons sent in and hauled into position, two and two across the drift, getting supports partly from the two inner sides of the waggons lashed together and strengthened, partly from low trestles placed inside the waggons, and at intervals along their outer sides.

In consequence of Captain Barrow's report of state of Amatikulu, the following Column order was issued to-day. 'The troops will remain at the present camp. To-morrow, two Companies Buffs, half Company Royal Engineers, under Captain Wynne, one Company Natal Pioneers, and four Companies Native Contingent, with as many tools as they can muster, escorted by a detachment of Mounted Infantry, will proceed at 8am to-morrow to the Amatikulu for the purpose of repairing the Drift.'

The Amatikulu was a challenge to Wynne's engineer training, and he had several ingenious plans in mind to improve the crossing. Pearson allowed him a large force of workmen from the Natal Native Contingent, who were expected to excel at manual labour – which British infantry notoriously loathed – rather than as fighting men.

¶ 'January 20th – We left at 8.15am with two Scotch carts[6] containing tools. A fine day, Mounted Infantry in front, followed by RE. We reached the

Amatikulu at 10am. The rain last night had made the drift still deeper, and as it was considered impassable, Colonel Pearson desired that another place of crossing should, if possible, be found and rendered practicable. I recommended that an attempt should be made to do this *at a point*, where the water, though running rather swiftly, was shallower, and the bottom, as far as was apparent from crossing on horseback, not bad, with the exception of a few stones. The approach could be made very good, that *on the far side* required the clearing away of boulders, but had the advantage of running directly to the onward road, avoiding a piece of very deep sand, and an ugly sharp turn. I proposed opening out a fresh channel to divert and diminish the current.

The Native Pioneers were employed making this channel, the Native Contingent removing the large boulders at the opposite bank. The Royal Engineers made the approach, cutting down the bank, making fascines, &c; and by handspikes, crowbars, jumpers &c,[8] and also some blasting with gun cotton,[9] removing the boulders from the bed of the river across the proposed new drift. This work proved a great deal more difficult of accomplishment than I had at first supposed. The men worked hard, but after four hours it became evident that we must not be dependent only upon this new undertaking; I therefore put on a large number to improve the old drift,(10) and also took a party of Royal Engineers and Natal Pioneers to improve the angle in the road and to widen the road beyond, which was in a deep cutting, only 5' to 5'6' at the bottom. Also laid fascines on the sandy approaches to the drift. At 4.45pm we left off and returned to the camp, $3^1/_2$ miles. An alarm at 10pm. Colonel Pearson complimented us upon our work to-day.'

¶ 'January 21st – Reveillé at 3.30am. The order of march changed for the future, the Royal Engineers always to follow the advanced guard, with a waggon of tools and stores, ready for any important affair in the roads, &c.
Arrived at Amatikulu at 6.30am. The river had gone down and the old drift was found passable. We crossed at 6.45. Very thick bush for 500 yards after crossing. After having advanced a mile, news came to us that the pole of the hospital waggon had been broken. I sent Corporal J Smith and Sapper O'Leary with tools to repair it.

Outspanned at 11am for breakfast. At noon an expedition sent out to reconnoitre Royal Kraal Indonduhla or Kinglae. Two Companies Buffs, some Naval Brigade, and the Royal Artillery returned, having seen a few stragglers, captured several fowls and burnt the Kraal.

Encamped at 4.30pm at Kwasamabela, 4 miles from Inyezane.'

The Royal Kraal burned on the 21st had been built by Cetshwayo in 1856 to commemorate his victory over a rival son of Mpande for the Zulu succession. It was more often known as Gingindhlovu - 'Gin-Gin-I-love-you' to the troops – and gave that name to Lord Chelmsford's own victory of April 2nd. The Zulus had abandoned the settlement save for a single old and senile woman, brought back by the raiding party, who had no idea where or why her people had gone, or, indeed, of anything else.

The Column had marched only seventeen miles in four days. It was hardly a lightning campaign.

NOTES

1) The official Précis reported that the Umsumdusi drift was $2^1/_2$ feet deep and 15 yards wide, with sandy banks 'about 8 feet high', and likely to 'deepen on account of high steep banks'. – *Précis of Information*, op cit, p 123.
2) 'The branches of the trees are inconveniently high, and the grass is very high.'
3) Captain – later Major – Percy Barrow, 19th Hussars (1848–86) commanded the mounted troops of No 1 Column, returned to Natal on Pearson's orders, and led Chelmsford's horsemen in the relief of Eshowe in April 1879. He later served in the 1st Boer War, the Egyptian campaign and the Gordon Relief Expedition.
4) 'Mealies' are the characteristic grain crop of Southern Africa, sometimes known to the British soldiery as 'kaffir corn'.
5) 'Corduroy' is a temporary road surface of logs placed side by side.
6) Light, two wheeled carts, usually drawn by mules.
7) Wynne probably made a sketch of the drift, showing the line of the original drift ('A–B'), together with his planned second drift ('C–D'), and channel ('E–F'). Pearson's staff officer, Captain McGregor, drew a series of excellent maps of landmarks along the Eshowe road, two of which are shown in Clarke's *Zululand at War*. If he made one of the Amatikulu, however, it has not survived.
8) Different types of hand tools.
9) Nitro-Cellulose, a smokeless explosive made by treating cotton with fuming nitric acid.
10) This probably covered the most difficult, stony-bottomed part of the drift.

Chapter Six: Inyezane – Into Battle

Wynne's next letter to Lucy was written on January 24th, the day after the column's arrival at Eshowe. It was his responsibility to turn the old mission house and buildings into a fortified position. Accordingly, he had reviewed the site and was about to begin the work of tracing out the lines of the fort. Since there was to be a courier – an African runner well paid for his courage – sent back to the Tugela camps, Wynne found a few minutes to tell his wife about his first battle:

¶ 'ESHOWE CAMP, Norwegian Mission Station, 37 miles from Tugela, 24th January – They are going to send a letter bag to the rear this afternoon, so I must write a hurried letter. As to keeping up a journal, it has been an impossibility. We march soon after daybreak always, and though we make slow progress each day's march, we do not get into camp till near dusk, and then there are duties which keep one hard at it till 'lights out'. We left the Tugela at 5am on the 18th to march into the enemy's country.

Two guns RA, two guns Naval Brigade, a Gatling and two rockets, a detachment of RA, the 2nd Company RE, the Buffs, a regiment of Mounted Infantry, about 100 Naval Brigade, two troops of Mounted Volunteers, a company of Native Pioneers, and four companies of Native Contingent (poor stuff!) – this, with 30 ox-waggons (16 oxen each), besides smaller mule waggons, formed the leading column, which was succeeded on the following day by another not so strong in troops, but with about 120 waggons.[1]

It poured with rain the night before we left, and also off and on, on our march. We marched to the opposite bank of the Inyoni, where we encamped for the night, and a wet business it was. Our routine is 'last post' at 8pm, when we have to turn in. Then at 3am we have to turn out under arms and fall in on our alarm posts, where we stand, chilled and often wet and sleepy, until daybreak. Then every third or fourth night there is an alarm from some outpost, and we have to turn out at a moments' notice in the dark – must sleep in one's clothes.

Our rations are pretty rough fare, and there is heaps of exercise for body and not a little for mind. However, I am, thank God, very well. I have had a little engineering work to do, and am now making a plan for the defences of this place, where they wish to establish a depot. The place is naturally very weak, and it will be an extremely difficult matter, and cannot, I fear, be satisfactory at the best.

And now, as time runs short, I must give you a hurried account of our first little battle, which took place the day before yesterday on the heights above the Inyezane Ford. We marched from our camping ground near the Amatikulu River at 5am. My company headed the column for the purpose of repairing bad places along the road. We came upon three swampy places one after another, at about one to half a mile apart, so that the company was split up for the time being.

At about 7.45 I brought up the portion last left behind and picked up the other two, so that we re-assembled at the Inyezane Ford. Meanwhile part of the column had gone on, and the leading portion had begun to 'out-span' for breakfast, when suddenly our scouts came upon about ten of the enemy, and a few minutes afterwards some hundreds made their appearance, and opened fire upon the head of our column. The road from the Inyezane runs up a steep hill, all the ground on that side being broken into spurs and deep ravines.

When I got my company together at the Inyezane I was just about to give them a short rest and some water, when suddenly we heard shots in the distance. I at once pushed forward along the road and saw the troops hotly engaged on the hill. The heights seemed swarming with Zulus, who were also shewing signs of working round the right flank so as to get at the waggons. I therefore determined to leave the road, and turned off to the right, and having reached a low narrow ridge, where I found the Mounted Infantry posted (on foot), I extended my company in skirmishing order from their (Mounted Infantry) right. We no sooner showed ourselves on the further slope of this ridge than the Zulus, who were concealed in the bush 150 to 250 yards off, began firing at us, bullets whizzing close by one, right and left. We returned it in good earnest and I selected places of cover behind trunks of trees, etc., for my men. After about a quarter of an hour some of the enemy retreated and others worked their way through the bush, so as further to try and outflank us. I extended the company, therefore, to wider intervals, and was glad to see immediately after a reinforcement come up from two companies of the Buffs, who extended themselves to our right. We then advanced upon the enemy through the bush, and after about an hour they were in full retreat, both those in front of us and those in the heights.

THE BATTLE OF INYEZANE

The Zulu army at Inyezane consisted of some 4–6,000 warriors under the command of Chief Godide kaNdlela Ntuli. Three Amabutho were present, the uMxhapo, iZingulube and uDlambedlu, as well as elements from the iQwa, inSukamngeni, uDududu and inDabawombe, and irregulars from the local Tonga peoples. The force was drawn up in position behind a long ridge known variously as Majia's Hill, 'Victory Hill' and Wombane. Three spurs ran down from the crestline towards the river Inyezane, each divided from the others by a ravine tangled with vegetation and marsh. John Dunn's road followed the central finger of Wombane, passing under a knoll on the right hand side. Further up the trail was a small kraal.

Godide's plan was to use the three spurs as paths for the wings and centre of the traditional Zulu attack, curling the left 'Horn' through the bush to catch the column in flank, while the 'Chest' struck Pearson's vanguard as it came up the road. These dispositions were good, and the army was fighting on the site of earlier victories. However, the impetuous valour of the young warriors was to throw the all-important timing out of sequence. While Colonel Pearson supervised the wagons crossing the drift, Zulu scouts were spotted on the bare knoll. A company of NNC went after them, chasing them across a ravine and onto the eastern finger. This action triggered a vigorous reaction by the left horn: instead of continuing to work its way around to the left, the mass of warriors stormed down the hill, overran the NNC, and alerted the British column at rest below. Pearson ordered his advance guard up the track, as he and his staff spurred their horses to the knoll which clearly dominated the riverward side of Wombane.

Two companies of the Buffs and 100 men of the Naval Brigade, with an impressive collection of weaponry, seized that landmark and opened up with artillery, rockets and the Gatling gun. Two more companies of the Buffs were sent out in open order to cover the exposed right flank of the column. Barrow's men were dismounted and forming a firing line: it was to extend this that Wynne and his command cast aside their picks and spades for Martini-Henrys. As the British fire grew hotter, the ardour of the left horn cooled, and the Zulus fell back. The skirmishing redcoats then advanced and pushed them into full-scale retreat. Meanwhile the Zulu chest had occupied the kraal, coming under heavy fire from the knoll.

As the huts went up in flames, Pearson counter-attacked with Bluejackets, Buffs and NNC. At this point the Zulu commanders seem to have decided the game was up. Their planned ambush had failed; the right horn had barely begun its manoeuvre, and the older Amabutho saw little reason to advance into combat once the British had gained the upper hand. At about 9.30am, an hour and a half after the battle had begun, the Zulu army quickly and tidily withdrew from the field, taking with it the dead and wounded.

Inyezane is something of a neglected battle in the history books. It took place on the same day as Isandhlwana and Rorke's Drift, and could hardly compete with them for the attention of the Victorian public. It was a victory – but scarcely a 'decisive' one, since the Zulus had withdrawn once the writing was on the wall. Yet the battle of Inyezane shows the British using modern open-order tactics to good effect; moving swiftly, attacking in skirmish lines and counter-punching towards the enemy centre once the Zulu assault had been broken. Pearson dealt with a very dangerous threat to his vulnerable column of wagons, with tremendous speed and clarity of vision – qualities which he showed neither before nor afterwards. Rather than adopt the defensive approach that later came to characterise British tactics against the Zulus and other African opponents, he used firepower in a flexible way: first breaking the enemy formations, and then himself attacking. In doing so he gained the initiative from Godide – whose response, quite sensibly, was to withdraw rather than gamble his veterans in an assault against an alerted and deployed enemy.

The fight lasted $2^1/_4$ hours.[2] I captured a shield and two assegais as trophies. I am thankful to say there were in my company no casualties, though one of my fellows had a narrow escape, the sight of his rifle being shot off. I am sorry to say the loss of our force was 9 killed and 14 wounded, and also several native allies. They lost, according to one of their chiefs who was made prisoner, about 300,[3] and their force numbered more than 4,000. They had certainly chosen a splendid position.

We afterwards marched on six miles and bivouacked for the night. Next we came here, where we remain ten days or more, to establish a depot.'

Wynne's statement that he had found it impossible to keep up a journal was not literally true, of course. He had been maintaining a professional diary - 'a semi-official one' as he referred to it in a later letter,[4] and 'very dry'. Certainly the diary was not written with a great deal of literary panache, nor did it cover every event in the detail the reader might wish – although sometimes the reverse is true, as the arcane jargon and calculations of the field engineer clutter the captain's prose. It was a precise, almost clinical document which casts a good deal of light on the drills and procedures of campaigning in the Victorian era. The entry for January 22nd is a lengthy one, and adds some hard facts to the previous, more florid, account:-

¶ 'ENGAGEMENT AT INYEZANE
January 22nd – Left Kwasamabela at 5am. Fine morning, Royal Engineers at head of Column, at two miles arrived at a bad swamp in road, left part of No. 4 section with tools to repair it, under Courtney and Willock. I took on the remainder, and at $2^1/_2$ miles came to a bad mud hole and water course, with irrigated mealie garden on either side at 6.44am. Detained about half the Company to repair it, with timber, brushwood, palm branches and sods. Courtney came up with those left before, and went on with remainder as far as the Inyezane, where was another bad place. At about 8am I came with the portion of the Company I had kept back, to the Inyezane stream, where I found the remainder. I was about to halt and give the men a rest when we heard firing about three-quarters of a mile off. I at once assembled the Company, and advanced quickly along the road till we came in view of the troops engaged on a spur from the high ground which rises immediately to the north of the Inyezane. The enemy showed in large numbers on the higher ground and appeared to be working round to the right flank of our Column of march. I therefore took my Company off to the right of the road to a low narrow ridge running south from the foot of the above mentioned

Map 5 - The Battle of Inyezane, 22nd January 1879

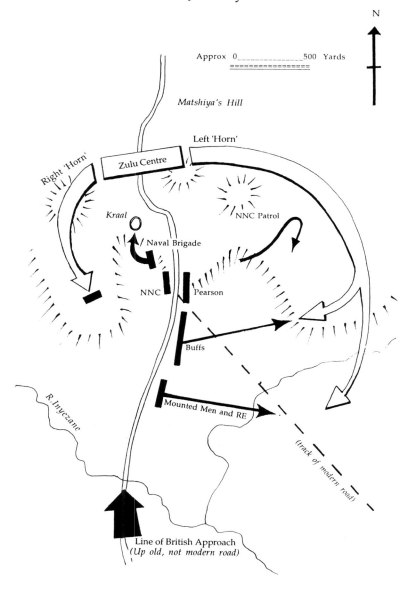

N

Approx 0_____500 Yards

Matshiya's Hill

Left 'Horn'

Right 'Horn'

Zulu Centre

Kraal

NNC Patrol

Naval Brigade

NNC

Pearson

Buffs

R. Inyezane

Mounted Men and RE

(track of modern road)

Line of British Approach
(Up old, not modern road)

spur. I found the Mounted Infantry, under Captain Barrow, already in occupation of a portion of this lower ground, so extended my Company in continuation of his right, but with my right thrown slightly forward along the further slope of this low ridge, keeping the men as far as practicable under cover.

We had no sooner arrived than the enemy, concealed in the bush on the slopes of the hills opposite to us, from 150 to 250 yards off, opened fire upon us, which we at once returned. After some minutes we observed several of the Zulus retreating up the hill sides, but fire was kept up by some, well-posted about 150 yards off, and there were signs of a further movement towards our right on the part of others. I extended my Company to the right to more open intervals, and about this time two Companies of the Buffs came up through the bush on our right rear and prolonged the line to our right. We then received the order to advance and clear the bush inclining to the right.

The Royal Engineers and two Companies of the Buffs then advanced across a stream and up the hill, through the bush, and then down a valley on the other side, gradually throwing forward the right. We advanced, crossing a spur, on which was a kraal, and then observed the enemy retreating quickly in large numbers, about 1,000 yards off. Uncertain whether we should continue our advance, Captain Harrison of the Buffs, the senior Officer then present, requested me to go back for instructions. These I obtained from Colonel Pearson, to the effect that the troops were to be brought back and the march continued. I accordingly brought in my Company round the foot of the intervening spurs (ie so as not to be visible by the enemy on the hills) and joined the Column of route.

Lieut. Main, RE, during this time, was detached from the RE and was acting with the 2nd Company Natal Native Pioneers. Shortly after crossing the Inyezane River, the pioneers were employed in repairing a portion of the road, and had just finished this and were pushing on again to repass the leading Company of the Buffs, the RA and Naval Brigade, when firing commenced between some of the Native Contingent and a few Kaffirs on their left. The fire at once grew rapid, and, by Col. Pearson's order, the two guns, RA, I Company Buffs, Naval Brigade, and the NN Pioneers, occupied the only commanding position in the vicinity, a small knoll commanded by the hills on three sides, and overlooking an undulating plain on the fourth. Immediately this position was taken up, the Zulus appeared on all the surrounding hills and commenced firing upon this knoll, which fire there was some difficulty in keeping down. The Pioneers, with their officers and Lieut. Main, RE, remained on this hill, with Colonel Pearson and Staff, till the termination of the action.

The number of officers and men of the Royal Engineers engaged were:-
Officers, 4, viz: Captain W Wynne. Lieuts D C Courtney, Main, and Willock.
Sergeants, 6. Rank and file, 86. No. of rounds expended, 1,850.[5]

The enemy consisted of the following regiments:[6]
Umdhleuefu, 1,000; Umkapu, 1,500; Ingulube, 500
District Military Kraals; Umgingindhlova, Isigwaka, Umangwe, Umkandhlu, about 1,500.   Total: 4,500.
Our loss was – Europeans, 8 killed and 9 wounded[7] (two died afterwards).
Natives, 6 killed.
The loss of the enemy was over 400.

The affair lasted about two hours. We then proceeded on our march and bivouacked for the night about 4 miles further on the road to Eshowe. One of our men had the sight of his rifle shot off.'

NOTES

1) Compare Wynne's figures with the official Narrative figures, as given in chapter five, above.
2) Other authorities claim that the battle lasted about 90 minutes; probably nobody timed the affair with any precision.
3) Zulu casualties are not known, but are generally placed at around 300 or 400.
4) That of February 18th.
5) About 20 rounds per man, fired over the course of at least an hour in action. Careful conservation of ammunition was essential to late nineteenth century warfare - 'rapid fire' was used only when faced with an assault at close quarters.
6) See the separate account of the battle of Inyezane for modern spellings of the names of the Amabutho. The four District Military Kraals were the stations for the local sections of the other regiments mentioned. Wynne gives no source for his numbers, but they appear convincing: Laband and Thompson's Field Guide to the War in Zululand (University of Natal, 1983) suggests that the local irregulars omitted in Wynne's listing comprised about 20% of the force – an addition of perhaps 800–1,000 men.
7) The strength of Pearson's force, and his losses, are shown below. The delay at the Amatikulu meant that part of Welman's detachment had come up before the leading column could move on, and thus men from both portions of No 1 Column fought at Inyezane. The source is Gerald French, Lord Chelmsford and the Zulu War (London, 1939):

Corps or Detachment		Officers	NCOs & Men
RA 11/7 (2 x 7 pdrs)		1	22
RE No 2 Company		4	85
2/3rd Regiment (5 coys)		11	400
99th Regiment (2 coys)		5	160
Naval Brigade (2 x 7 pdr, 1 Gatling,1 rocket tube)		6	128
No 2 Squadron Mounted Infantry		5	115
Natal Hussars		2	37
Stanger Mounted Rifles		2	35
Victoria Mounted Rifles		2	45
2nd Regiment NNC	1st battalion	28	800
	2nd battalion	27	800
No 2 Coy Natal Native Pioneers		2	60

Casualties:

Corps or detachment	Killed Officers	NCO/Men	Wounded Officers	NCO/Men	Remarks
2/3rd	–	2	–	5	Incl. 1 died of wounds
Naval Brigade	–	–	–	7	Cols Pearson &
Mtd Infantry	–	–	–	2	Parnell each had
Native Contingent	{Lt JL Raines {Lt J Platterer	6	Lt H Webb	1	their horses shot from under them

---

VOICES FROM INYEZANE

There are a number of personal accounts of the battle of Inyezane apart from those of Warren Wynne. This is how it looked to some of the men who were there:-

They came down a ravine on each side of the hill, and right over the top of it, attempting to surround our columns, and on the first shot being fired our native levies skedaddled and left their officers, five of whom were shot before you could look round. Directly they were down, the Kaffirs were upon them, and assegaied them cruelly, stabbing them in twenty or thirty places...

They came on with an utter disregard of danger. The men that fired did not load the guns. They would fire and run into the bush, and have fresh guns loaded for them, and out again. They fire young cannon balls, slugs and even gravel. I tell you what it is: our 'school' at Chatham, over one hot whiskey, used to laugh about these niggers, but I assure you that fighting with them is terribly earnest work, and not child's play.

Colour Sergeant J W Burnett, 99th regiment [1]

I heard firing at the front. I immediately pushed forward, when I found the advance guard hotly engaged. The staff, Lloyd's guns, some of the Buffs, and the bluejackets occupied a low knoll to the right of the road; in front of them was a high hill overlooking our position, in possession of the Zulus. The mounted men were on a plain to the right, and the road was completely commanded by the enemy, who were concealed over the ridge of their hill, and kept up a heavy fire.

Unidentified Officer, Naval Brigade [2]

The fight lasted from three to four hours, hard fighting. I am thankful to say I escaped. We expect another battle in a few days. We were taken by surprise in the bush.

Sapper Thomas Cullern, 2nd Field Company RE [3]

I crossed the Tugela on the 15th January into the enemy's country and had a severe engagement on the 22nd and defeated them with the loss of 800 of the enemy, who all ran away, and we went after them up country and bivouacked for the night.

Private Joseph Morgan, 2/24th Regiment, detached for mounted duty.[4]

The Zulus awaited us in a very well-chosen spot – high, bare and very steep hills in our front, bush and swamp on our right, and steep hills on our left... there was nothing approaching to a scramble, but a regular orderly series of manoeuvres on both sides and increased the interest of the day's proceedings.

Captain H G MacGregor, 29th Regiment [5]

The whites shot us down in numbers, in some places our dead and wounded covered the ground, we lost heavily, especially from the small guns (ie small arms), many of our men were drowned in the Nyezane river.

Sihlahla, warrior in the uMxhapho regiment[6]

We went forward packed close together like a lot of bees... we were still far away from them when the white men began to throw their bullets at us, but we could not shoot at them because our rifles would not shoot so far... We never got nearer than 50 paces to the English, and although we tried to climb over our fallen brothers we could not get very far ahead because the white men were firing heavily close to the ground into our front ranks while the 'by-and-by' was firing over our heads into the regiments behind us... The battle was so fierce that we had to wipe the blood and brains of the killed and wounded from our heads, faces, arms, legs and shields after the fighting.

Zinema, warrior in the uMxhapho regiment[7]

Cetshwayo was very angry with Godide, who was commanding the older regiments, the uDlambedlu and iZingulube, for not taking a more active part in the fight. It is said they merely looked on, and took no part at all.

'Ndobolongwana', reporting his brother Nombona [8]

References

1) Frank Emery *The Red Soldier* p.185
2) Ibid p.186
3) Ibid p.187
4) Ibid p.188
5) Sonia Clarke, *Zululand at War* p.148
6) John Laband *Fight Us in the Open*, (Pietermaritzburg, 1985) p.27
7) Ibid p.27
8) Ibid p.25

Chapter Seven: Eshowe I - 'A Very Awkward Position'

The next step of the campaign was to reach Eshowe and fortify the mission site as a depot for supplies. Colonel Pearson thought it vital to follow up the victory at Inyezane immediately, so that the Zulus would not believe they had inflicted a check on the progress of No.1 Column. As CRE, Warren Wynne was to take a key role in the fortification of Eshowe; he rode ahead to reconnoitre the position:-

¶ 'January 23rd – The day after the affair at Inyezane we left our bivouack at 5am, RE and Natal Pioneers leading. We repaired four bad places along the road within the first $2^1/_2$ miles, after which the road as far as Eshowe was good. Eshowe lies about $1^1/_2$ miles off the road. It has been a Norwegian Mission Station,[1] but was abandoned several months ago when these troubles began. There are three thatched buildings built of sun-dried bricks and plastered – one a dwelling-house with verandah and several small rooms, one a school-room, and a third containing a workshop and store-rooms. There is a church built of similar material, but with corrugated iron roof, with vestry at east end. These buildings lie on ground sloping from west to east, the church being on the higher ground; the dwelling-house, with a good garden and orange grove, is on the lower part of the slope, at the bottom of which runs a stream of water, well supplied by springs from all sides. This stream runs in a south-easterly direction and is met by another small watercourse on the south side of the Station. On the rising ground beyond these two watercourses, stand three other small houses with gardens containing orange trees, banana, pines, &c. The valley of the stream and the whole vicinity of the station is wooded and thickly grown with underwood. The station stands high as regards the surrounding country generally, but is commanded by hills, from 400 to 1200 yards distant on the north and south sides, to the extent of 20ft to 30ft in places. To the west of the station, about 70 yards from the church, the ground falls suddenly and forms a deep kloof, with bush. The approach by the road is along a narrow ridge running a short distance from north-west to south-east past the station, otherwise the ground falls away from it on all sides.

This station had been selected as a depot for stores for our column, and also of the others which it is intended shall concentrate upon Ulundi (King

Cetshwayo's kraal) from Rorke's Drift, Utrecht and Middleberg.

It was chosen (from description merely) on account of its position as regards distance from the Lower Tugela, the ample supply of water and healthiness of site, but chiefly because of the buildings existing ready for occupation as store-rooms. When within 2 miles of this place Colonel Pearson and his staff, with an escort of mounted men, rode forward to inspect it. I accompanied him, and after we had ridden round it expressed my opinion that the position itself was weak and subject to great disadvantages in a military point of view, and that had we but brought with us the materials for erecting a store (similar to that at the Lower Tugela) it would have been preferable to have selected the more open and commanding ground to the north of Eshowe. It was now, however, too late. Shelter for the stores was required without delay; there was no timber even growing, suitable for building, and there was nothing for it but to utilize the buildings ready to our hands and do all that was possible, with the means at our disposal, to put the place in a state of defence. A special request[2] had been made that the orange trees might be left standing, which had been acceded to by the Colonel commanding. I then rode down to the stream with Captain MacGregor, AQMG, to arrange about the water supply. The troops arrived and were encamped on the two ridges running south-west and north-west from the church, and between which lies the kloof before mentioned. My company was encamped within the station in front of the buildings, and the Head Quarters at the top of the garden in rear of the dwelling house. At night the garden was occupied by a strong picquet of the Buffs.'

¶ 'January 24th – A strong party employed clearing the bush close round the station. We determined the trace of the work to be occupied by a small garrison of about 400 men to protect the stores, and commenced making profiles. Found it absolutely necessary to cut down the orange trees.

The proposed trace of the work, which was restricted as far as the positions of the buildings would allow, had a perimeter of 400 yards. It was not by any means such as would have been selected had we not been compelled to take all the buildings in. An alarm at night.'

On the 24th the remaining detachment, under Lt Col Welman, marched in. Work on the fort was in full swing, the Royal Engineers handling the complex tasks and supervising the manual labour of the infantry, sailors and NNC. On three successive nights the new garrison was awakened by 'alarms'; the soldiers were evidently nervous, even before news of disaster elsewhere in Zululand arrived.

¶ 'January 25th – Working party consisted of RE 50, Natal Native Pioneers 40, and Native Contingent 250, for 8 hours; 2 companies Buffs 90, and Naval Brigade 50, for 6 hours.

RE employed profiling, felling timber, tracing and superintending, &c; 1 Co. Buffs, Naval Brigade, and Natal Pioneers, excavating south ditch; 1 Co. Buffs and Native Contingent felling and clearing. Major Coates and convoy of empty waggons sent down with three companies to Tugela.[3] An alarm at night.'

¶ 'Sunday, January 26th – News received by a 'runner' of a defeat of the force of Col. Durnford, RE, on the 22nd inst., which it was said was obliged to fall back after severe loss, and that Col. Durnford had been killed. That, on the other hand, the General had gained a victory over the enemy.[4]

Working party the same as yesterday. Commenced revetting the south face with hurdle revetment. Commenced excavating north face. Col. Pearson having drawn my special attention to the question of defilading the interior from the hill to the north, I had the profile at the re-entering angle of north face made to give a crest of 8'6' above the ground, running to 7' at the north-east angle, and 6' at the north-west angle – 6ft being the relief of the remainder of the work.

Working party employed as yesterday: RE 6 hours, remainder 3 hours. At 11.45pm we turned out for an 'alarm', which proved, as usual, of an insignificant nature. Divine Service at 10am by Rev – Robinson,[5] Chaplain to the Column (Missionary in Zululand and Natal from S.P.G.)'[6]

The 'news' brought by the runner was a note from Sir Bartle Frere, despatched in haste from Pietermaritzburg. As far as anyone at Eshowe knew, Colonel Durnford's command was still in reserve at Middle Drift, thirty miles upstream from No 1 Column's bases at the mouth of the Tugela. Thirty miles was an easy day's journey for a victorious Impi, which might then fall on the forts or the wagon convoy presently in transit.

A second messenger arrived, bearing word from Lt Kingscote RN, commanding at Fort Tenedos. His post had come under heavy, if ineffective, fire on the night of the 25th. The Zulus had vanished into the darkness after an hour's shooting.

These tidings meant that Fort Eshowe had to be made complete and defensible at once. Wynne's reference to Pearson's concern over defilade fire – fire into the backs of the defenders from overlooking hills – marks the realisation that Eshowe was now more than a supply dump. In the Diary entry of 27th January, Captain Wynne assessed the current strength of his command:-

¶ 'January 27th – Strength of 2nd Co. RE –
Working party, RE and Natal Native Pioneers for 8 hours, and 1 Company Buffs, 40 Naval Brigade, and 250 Native Contingent for 6 hours.

	Officers	Sergts	Drivers	Horses & R&F
Hd. Qrs., Eshowe)	3	86	6	12 (1 sick)
Attached	1 [7]			
Cape Town	1			
Durban	1 [8]	5	15	
Lower Tugela		7		

Ammunition, 160 rounds per man, including 50 on the person.

Proceeded with revetment of south and north faces; the excavation of south face about three-parts finished; ditch of a caponier on that face begun. Revetment of north face begun; excavation proceeded with. Excavation east faces and stockade commenced. Clearing in front of east faces, in kloof in front of west face, and along streams to north-east and south of work proceeded with. 55 RE felling timber, profiling, working at stockade and superintending.

Preparations made for using 4 waggons lined with tarpaulin for holding water as reserve tanks. Small brick building at north-east angle loop-holed, and thatched roof plastered by RE.[9]

Demolished (partly with gun cotton) two houses on hill 300 yards from fort.'

On the 28th a messenger brought word from Lord Chelmsford: a vague but evidently deadly earnest telegram which began, 'The unfortunate disaster which has occurred to No 3 Column has, I fear, placed you in a very awkward position... ' It stated that no support could be sent to Pearson until reinforcements arrived from England, adding the hope that the Zulus would obligingly 'knock their heads' against the walls of Eshowe. Chelmsford's optimism that the Amabutho would come and receive a stern lesson at the hands of No 1 Column seems unlikely to have been shared by the recipients of the cable, especially in view of the final paragraph:

¶ 'Consider all my instructions as cancelled, and act in whatever manner you think most desirable in the interests of the column under your command. Should you consider the garrison of Eshowe as too far advanced to be fed with safety, you can withdraw it. Hold, however, if possible, the post on the Zulu side of the lower Tugela. You must be prepared to have the whole Zulu force down on you. Do away with tents, and let the men take shelter under the wagons which will then be in position for defence and hold so many more supplies.'

Colonel Pearson called a conference of his officers to discuss the issues at hand. They were to decide whether to abandon Eshowe and make a run for the Tugela, with precious little information upon which to base their decision. The Council of War was by no means a normal institution in Victorian campaigning. Those few times of crisis that had caused

---

ISANDHLWANA AND RORKE'S DRIFT

The events in the Central Column on 22nd January are the subject of great speculation in Wynne's letters. What happened on that day that so changed the course of the campaign?

The Battle of Isandhlwana is one of the best-known disasters in British military history. It was the consequence of several separate errors, which united to create a situation where the Zulus were able to catch the Imperial forces in their most vulnerable state. Chelmsford received word of an enemy sighting from his forward patrols. He took the bulk of No 3 Column to reinforce the vanguard, in the hope of forcing a battle. Left at his HQ at the stores depot of Isandhlwana (a prominent natural rock outcrop), was a garrison of six companies of the 24th Foot; 2 guns;115 mounted infantry & volunteers, and 431 men of the Natal Native Contingent. The camp remained unfortified, despite standing orders and much advice, because of the need to move wagons back and forth along the line of communication. There was a division in command between Lt Col Pulleine of the 1/24th – who had been left as base commander – and Col Durnford, his superior in rank, who arrived with his force of mounted Sotho during the morning of the 22nd. This confusion of responsibility and planning served to make a dangerous situation more dangerous still.

The main Zulu army was not, as Chelmsford believed, some miles ahead – but close at hand, resting in a valley below the nQutu plateau, immediately to the north of the camp. The Impi had not been ordered to attack the depot, but when a Sotho horseman chanced to discover it, its reaction was to launch an immediate assault from the uplands towards the camp below. Pulleine underestimated the strength of the attack, and drew his companies out in a thin firing line a mile from his tents, while Durnford advanced his men eastward across the valley towards Chelmsford's assumed position. The stretched defenders were assailed by some 20,000 warriors, who were at first held in check by disciplined volley fire. Durnford's men, however, were forced to retire when they ran out of ammunition. Pulleine moved a company of the 24th to cover the retreat: but the sudden onrush of Zulus was overwhelming. The NNC broke as they were attacked on two sides, and the the regulars – who may themselves have been running low on ammunition – were either killed where they stood, or pushed back into the camp in small knots of men. Durnford fell in a 'gallant last stand', while the drifts of the Buffalo River became clogged as the Zulu right horn swung around to cut off the fugitives. Only 55 of the 950 Europeans survived, and most of the NNC were cut down. Zulu losses were also grievous – perhaps 2,000 killed and wounded. When Lord Chelmsford returned after dark, he was faced by a scene of carnage, and the total loss of all supplies, transport and animals.

Rorke's Drift was the immediate result of Isandhlwana. The far right of the Zulu army had not been engaged in the slaughter at the camp and at the Buffalo crossings, but carried on towards the old Swedish mission station of Rorke's Drift. This consisted of two large buildings, now in use as a store and a hospital, garrisoned by 'B' Company, 2/24th, together with a company of NNC and various detached troops from other units. The overall commander was Lt John Chard RE, who was present to supervise the building of a pont across the Blood River at the drift. The news of Isandhlwana arrived around 3.30, as fugitives ran panting in from north and east. Within the hour, Zulus were taking up positions on all sides of the site, and the NNC had taken off in full flight. This left a force of 139 officers and men, 35 of them patients sick in the hospital. Chard and his officers had fortified the mission buildings with loopholes and barricades, forming an outer perimeter with mealie bags, biscuit boxes and two wagons. There was also an inner redoubt of biscuit boxes.

The Zulu force consisted of perhaps 4,000 men of the uNdi corps (uThulwana, inDluyenge and unDhlondlo regiments) under Dabulamanzi, with elements of Zibhebu's uDloko. The first assault was from the south, covered by fire from Zulu riflemen on the terraces of the hill known as the Oskarberg. The British fire halted the attack at 50 yards, the Zulus streaming around the hospital to their left, and coming in again at the north-west angle. Throughout the evening the warriors attacked again, hitting the hospital and the north wall. About 7pm the hospital became untenable as the roof caught fire and the defenders were forced to fall back – dragging patients through holes cut in the interior walls, as Zulus broke in and speared those unable to escape.

The redoubt saved the garrison. All night the fighting raged, illuminated by the still-burning hospital. About 4am there was a lull, as the Zulus faded back into the darkness. Dabulamanzi had disobeyed orders by attacking the mission, and his gamble had failed. At dawn the defenders found themselves alone amongst the dead and wounded. British losses were 17 killed and 8 wounded: Zulu casualties are unknown, but 370 bodies were counted in the immediate vicinity of Rorke's Drift.

Eleven Victoria Crosses were awarded for the defence of Rorke's Drift, more than for any other single action in British history. Critics suggested that this bounty was designed to cover the humiliation of Isandhlwana, and probably it was. This battle was, after all, a very minor skirmish in a small colonial war. For all that, however, it appeared as a blessed deliverance from a Zulu invasion of Natal. The unquestionable heroism of the defenders became a model for Victorian Britons of how their soldiers were expected to conduct themselves.

commanders to summon a meeting where the officers would select a plan by voting – such as the beleaguered Kabul garrison of 1841–2, or the besieging force at Delhi in 1857 – had been notable for confusion, indecision, and a general failure of direction.

Wynne's firm position in favour of retaining the Eshowe post was based on the strength of the works in progress, and on the psychological importance of holding on. To stay meant that, despite his victory of the 22nd, Cetshwayo would still have a force of redcoats entrenched inside his territory.[10] To retreat meant, at the very least, conceding the initiative to the Zulus, starting a panic among the civilian population of Natal, and a further decline in British standing among the subject tribes. At worst, a run for the Tugela might mean being caught on the road, and overwhelmed by the architects of Chelmsford's 'Unfortunate Disaster'. The Zulu army could then strike into Natal at will. Wynne was clearly right – and proved persuasive – as did the news, which arrived during the council, that Colonel Ely's convoy was less than ten miles from Eshowe.

Cross Section of the Walls at Fort Eshowe

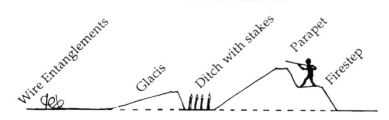

¶ 'January 28th – Commenced work at 6am. Worked $9^1/_2$ hours. Working party about same strength. At 10am telegram[11] received from General Lord Chelmsford hinting at the occurrence of a disaster, and stating he had found it necessary to retire to the frontier, that all former plans had been given up, that Colonel Pearson must expect the whole Zulu force to bear down upon his Column, and leaving him full discretion to retire upon the Tugela or to hold his position.

At a meeting of Commanding Officers, to which I was called, I found it had been pretty well determined to retreat at once, leaving all standing. The fort being in a tolerable advanced state, I could not concur in this decision, looking upon such retreat as hazardous in itself, and the moral effect of it to be greatly deprecated. I therefore was in favour of remaining and strengthening our position to the utmost. It was, however, a question of provisions and ammunition, and about the sufficiency of these for holding out for any length of time there was some uncertainty. At this point Col Walker, AAG, and Capt. MacGregor, AQMG, came in, and being decidedly of the same opinion as myself, the question was again opened, and after a short discussion it was determined to remain, sending back to the Tugela the mounted troops, viz: Mounted Infantry and Volunteers, and also the Native Contingent (2 battalions). All tents were struck. We worked hard all day. There was, however, something of a panic and the parapets and revetments suffered severely in consequence. The profiles were almost all knocked down and the required height for defence obtained, by heaping on the already excavated earth, sacks and boxes of provisions, men's valises[12] and blankets, tents, tent bags, &c. I had proposed that the waggons (loaded) should be brought inside and parked lengthwise, parallel to and about 10 yards in rear of the crests of the parapets of every face, so as to act as traverses from reverse fire. The remainder parked down the centre west to east. The conductors, however, performed this clumsily, running some almost into the parapets and cramping and hampering the space needed for work.

It was impossible for the 4 RE Officers to maintain a proper supervision while all this confusion went on – and undoubtedly it will have a deteriorating effect upon the work, besides entailing much additional labour afterwards. Loopholes, within about a foot of the eaves of the roof, were made in all the walls of the church, also galleries for marksmen. The church windows were stopped up with cornsacks, &c., it being intended for a hospital. Platforms were made for 4 guns (2 RA and 2 RN 7 pdrs) and a Gatling (RN), and these mounted (pro tem).[13] The caponier was discontinued for the present.

At 6.30pm our anxiety was greatly relieved by the arrival of a convoy of provisions in 72 waggons, with 3 Cos 99th and 2 Cos Buffs,[14] under Lt-Col.[15] Ely, 99th Regt.

As these waggons had to be disposed of and the cattle protected, I proposed the formation of a 'laager' of waggons to contain the oxen on the south glacis. This was carried out and formed before dark, the lines being laid out as in sketch,[16] which caused the least masking of fire.

Was called up at 11.30pm, the church tower being on fire, which had been caused by one of the Sappers having endeavoured to smoke out a nest of bees there during the afternoon and left some smouldering straw. Sent two Sappers up and had buckets of water hauled up from inside the church by them. The fire was put out before midnight – no damage of consequence.

Dissension amongst brother officers, alarm in the camp and destruction of his partially finished work, capped by a sudden fire in the mission chapel: the Diary notes these events with cool detachment. Warren Wynne's state of mind was probably rather less glacial, however, as is shown by the letter he wrote to Lucy:-

¶ 'ESHOWE FORT, 28th January 1879 – My own darling wife, Perhaps at the same time as you receive this you will read in the newspapers some bad news of the expedition into Zululand; at least Colonel Pearson has to-day received a telegram from the General commanding, which was not explicit, but full of ill forebodings, leaving Colonel Pearson free to retreat at once to the frontier, as it was expected that the whole Zulu force would be down upon our column, and that the other columns (so we must gather) had gone back; at any rate, that we must look for no help.

It was at first decided to retreat at once. I was one of the minority to insist on remaining, as I looked upon a retreat of 37 miles as likely to be most disastrous. It has been decided to remain and fight to the last. Our provisions will suffice for some time with care; and though ammunition is rather scarce, I hope it will last, if they only send some force to our relief. My fort is more than half finished, and we are straining every energy to complete it, at any rate roughly, by to-night.

Do not trouble your heart, my darling. Hope the best; and if I am taken, it will be, through God's mercy, into His Paradise of Love. To Him I commend you, my own sweet precious wife, and my darling children. Love to all dear ones.

Your fond husband, WARREN WYNNE

In the original edition of the Letters, Lucy inserted a few words of her own at this point:-

¶ 'After some hesitation and reluctance I decided on copying this last letter word for word, as I felt I should not otherwise express its simple trustful courage, its resignation and affection. But I have, as a rule, strictly avoided repeating any of my husband's more affectionate words and messages, feeling them too sacred for any eyes but my own, though I fear I have thereby necessarily failed to express fully the deeply religious tone of his writing.'

1) The mission at Eshowe was founded by Osmund Oftebro (1820–93), a Norwegian who had been active in Zululand since 1849. His son Martin played an important role in the capture of Cetshwayo in August 1879.
2) By Mr Oftebro.
3) This convoy consisted of 48 empty wagons and, according to Morris (*Washing of the Spears* p.427), an escort of four rather than three companies – two each of the Buffs and the 99th.
4) These apparently conflicting pieces of information referred, of course, to the actions of Isandhlwana and Rorke's Drift respectively.
5) The Reverend Robert Robertson – not Robinson – was a Scotsman of 58 years: a High Church Anglican who had been ordained in 1860. He had founded four mission stations in Zululand. His wife, tragically killed in a wagon accident in 1861, was buried in Eshowe churchyard.
6) The Society for the Propagation of the Gospel.
7) Lieutenant Main RE.
8) Lieutenant Haynes (last mentioned waiting for the pontoons to arrive by sea) never did reach No 1 Column. He accompanied Chelmsford's relief force, and later – as we shall see – was responsible for opening communications with Eshowe by heliostat.
9) The plastering was to prevent any possibility of the thatch catching fire.
10) Unknown to the officers of No 1 Column, Evelyn Wood was laagered far to the north-west, at Kambula Hill, with his own No 4 Column.
11) The electric telegraph extended as far as Fort Pearson, from whence the runner was sent. Lord Chelmsford had despatched it from Pietermaritzburg, his headquarters following the collapse of his central column's advance.
12) The valise was a black lacquered canvas case for personal kit, issued to rank and file at this period. It replaced the older model of knapsack from 1871 onwards.
13) Pro Tempore – ie "For the Moment.'
14) Morris (p.428) adds two companies of NNC to this escort.
15) Abbreviation for 'Lieutenant Colonel'.
16) No sketch remains.

Chapter Eight: Eshowe II – Under Siege

Eshowe was ablaze with activity. Percy Barrow led the mounted volunteers out of the camp on the afternoon of the 29th, followed by the levies of the 2nd NNC. The landscape teemed with bands of Zulus, watching from ridges and tailing the column at a safe distance. There was no attempt at attack, but Barrow sensibly pushed on to the Tugela. Putting spurs to horses, the riders were at Fort Tenedos by midnight. The Natal blacks, unable to keep up with horsemen, began to fall behind. Morale and discipline cracked as the leading companies broke into a trot. The men rushed towards Tenedos – or made for the cover of the hills – as seemed best to each individual, leaving the European officers bemused and discouraged in the roadway. The Zulus left them all alone, and penny packets of the NNC straggled into the fort throughout January 30th. The departure of Barrow's column meant that the Eshowe garrison of 1,357 combat troops and 337 civilian voorloopers and conductors had a little more room – though hardly enough. Wolseley[1] recommended a space of 150 x 120 yards (18,000 square yards) for an infantry battalion using tents, in a restricted space –and ideally some 85,000 square yards. At Eshowe more than double that number of people were to be housed, under wagons, in only 10,000 square yards. The sanitary risks were to show themselves very quickly, and Warren Wynne's diary indicates something of the state of affairs:-

¶ 'January 29th – Worked about 8 hours. Much inconvenience from crowding of waggons and the spoiling of parapets done yesterday. Excavation of ditches proceeding all round. An alarm at mid-day. Parapets again roughly handled. Much confusion with working parties. Work proceeding under great disadvantages.'

On January 29th a runner brought a sack of letters from home, including one from Lucy Wynne; but no news of the war.

¶ 'January 30th – 900 head of cattle sent back to Tugela with native drivers. These we afterwards learnt fell into the enemy's hand.

Was taken ill with billious diarrhoea from exposure to sun, and perhaps anxiety. Was forced to lie down nearly all day.'

The loss of the oxen was a most serious matter. There was no pasturage at Eshowe to feed the 1,200 draught animals, but they would be crucial if the column were to move out in any direction. If Pearson sent them back to the Tugela forts, however, he would be able to send down a force to retrieve them later: not an ideal plan, but perhaps the best available. As things turned out, he sent some 900² cattle under escort of the remaining company of NNC. Within an hour the Native Contingent was back – minus the oxen. The Zulus had attacked and simply chased off the Natal men, the better to seize the treasure trove of cattle. This was a blow for Pearson, since at 8 animals per vehicle, it meant that more than 100 of his wagons would be immobilised. If he was to retire to the Natal side of the river, it would be at the price of abandoning much of his stores.

The Diary entries show the concern of the moment:

¶ 'January 31st – Weak after yesterday. Reveillé 4.30am. Out lights, 8pm. Visit to sentries 1am. Stand to arms, 3.30am.'

¶ 'Feb 1st – To-day we commenced shortened rations.'

There was more news on February 2nd:

¶ 'Runners arrived from Lower Tugela with despatch for the General giving some details of the disaster at Isandhlwana on the 22nd ult. Colonel Pearson sent a despatch to the General with a general plan of the work. An alarm at 9.30pm.'

The letters brought in gave enough information to provide a picture of what had happened at Isandhlwana on the 22nd. Pearson wrote to Chelmsford asking for seven companies of reinforcements. Wynne told his wife all he knew:-

¶ 'ESHOWE, 4th February 1879 – There is a chance of getting a letter carried through the enemy's country and scouts by means of a native runner, so I will snatch a few moments from constant work to write you a few lines. I am dreading the anxiety you will, I know, experience when you hear of the terrible disaster which befell one of our columns on the very day that the column to which I am attached gained a victory over the Zulus. Lord Chelmsford had advanced to engage the enemy in his front, leaving his camp with 600 Europeans to guard it. These latter, when he had advanced a

Map 7 - Fort Eshowe

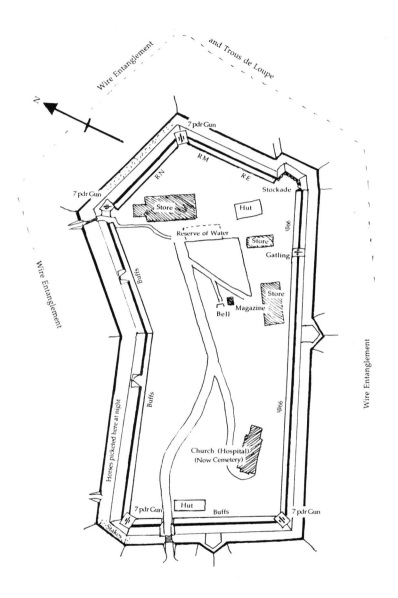

few miles, were suddenly attacked by 20,000 Zulus, whom they heroically resisted for four hours, when ammunition failed and all but about 70 or 80 were killed, including 30 officers. Both our officers with the column were killed. Is it not heart-rending? Lord Chelmsford sent to Colonel Pearson to give him free liberty of action, to retreat to the Tugela or not. We have decided to remain, and have been working with might and main to fortify this position, unfortunately a naturally weak one, but necessary to hold, because of the buildings used as stores for the expedition. We may any day expect the whole Zulu force upon us, and cannot expect to be relieved for three or four weeks at least.

We have about five weeks' rations, which we are eking out, so as to last longer; and, with God's help, I have no fear but that we shall hold out and withstand any number of the enemy, and that our doing so will be a very great advantage to future operations is undoubted. It has been a great strain and source of immense anxiety to me to bear the responsibility of carrying out this large work under so many disadvantages – surrounded by quantities of bush, affording dangerous cover, all which had to be cleared; commanded on three sides by hills, and with the difficulties caused by the stoppages of work through frequent alarms of the supposed approach of the enemy. One's rest at night is interrupted nightly by these, and one has to rise and be under arms daily at 3.30am We are now on short rations; nevertheless, except for two days, my health has been excellent, and I am continually thanking God for all His mercies. A former missionary of this benighted land is our chaplain. We have had Divine Service once a week, and are to have the Holy Communion (DV)[3] next Sunday.

Your letter of the 12th December reached me on the 29th ultimo, the day after I sent off my last, when we had first heard a report of the disaster. We have not slept in tents since that day, but bivouacked under waggons, etc.

My fort is nearly completed. It is now quite safe enough, but some few important finishing touches have to be given.

I am keeping a diary as well as I can, and will have a long letter written ready to send off when there is a good opportunity, but at present every moment of time is devoted to the superintendence of the many parts of this work. My officers work admirably.

Your letter, and Flo's, and May's, and my darling little Arthur's,[4] were a treat and a comfort to me beyond all description. My missionary friend has told me I must close this up. May God's blessing be upon you and ours, and all dear ones.'

On the 6th a runner panted up the track. He bore two despatches from Lord Chelmsford, dated February 2nd and 4th. The general reported that he had no forces to spare for Eshowe, and suggested a partial retirement at least. The loss of the oxen had seriously weakened Pearson's ability to do this, at least without making an undignified run for safety. He replied offering to send back the three companies of the 99th, and most of the civilians, in return for three companies of his own regiment. He added that any move at all on his part would require 20 wagons' of food, with full spans of trek-oxen. At this point both Chelmsford and Pearson appear to have been at a loss what to do and, communicating by a precarious stream of messengers, were groping blindly for the answer. The runner was able to carry letters back to Natal, so Wynne once again put pen to paper on the 7th:-

¶ I hear there is another chance of sending off a letter this evening; also that the 'runner' who went down to the Tugela three nights ago arrived there, though he was nearly captured on two occasions by parties of the enemy's scouts. I hope this letter may be equally successful.

We are still strengthening the Fort, and I begin to have great confidence in it, both for its offensive powers as well as for its defensive and protective.

There ought hardly to be a casualty from the fire from outside; and even if they come in many thousands and persevere in spite of heavy losses to the edge of the ditches, I don't think they will find it easy to get in. I am now beginning to make a variety of obstacles to check their advance should they arrive within thirty yards of the place: – Shallow little pits, with stakes at the bottom chequer-wise; entanglements of wire; and, by-and-by, explosive traps.

It has been heart-breaking to be compelled to make a wilderness of this spot which was so beautiful before, with its orange grove and gardens of flowers, lovely arums, and royal ferns, growing like trees. But I had to have acres of bush and timber cut down all round to prevent cover for any enemy approaching. Colonel Pearson is very kind, and is pleased with our work.

This place was a Norwegian Mission Station. The church we have turned into a hospital, but alas! I had to have it loopholed. Of course we shall repair it when the war is over. Ah! when? I wish I could know that two or three months would see the end of it, but it is impossible to say.

Lord Chelmsford is obliged to wait for reinforcements, and meanwhile our column within this fort must remain as the occupants of Zululand, the others having retired to the frontier. We are 37 miles by road from the Tugela. We are on short rations, but not, I think, insufficient, and I expect there is enough for five weeks at least, with ordinary care, and doubtless before that we shall have a convoy of provisions up.

We are all, thank God, in good health. The weather is beautiful; the air delightful, except in parts where one gets too much 'bouquet' of oxen or horses. Of course every precaution of a sanitary nature is taken as far as can be.

We had news yesterday from the Tugela. It appears that those poor fellows who were massacred by the 20,000 Zulus on the 22nd were straggling within a mile of their camp, getting wood, water etc., and were taken by surprise, while the General was advancing some miles off against a smaller body of the enemy, who evidently drew him off on purpose. We also hear that one Company only of the 1/24th Regt. (80 men) were engaged with 2,500 of the enemy for twelve hours, held their ground almost without losing a man, and killed 370 of the enemy (at Rorke's Drift). The first poor fellows were not watchful enough; the last were on their guard.

Your letter of the 12th January[5] was just what I like, so that I can picture our dear home and all the dear ones, and your various doings. Pray thank all our kind friends for their kind enquiries, which I appreciate very much indeed. I am rejoiced to hear such good accounts of our youngest pet; he will have grown out of my recollection when I see him next. Kiss him many times, and each of the darlings for me, and thank Arthur for his very nice letter, and tell him I am building a large castle, and towers to shoot the enemy from, with a deep ditch all round it. Darling little Harry, too; how I long to see him.

I feel the responsibility of the work very much, and occasionally have small trials of temper from contrarieties of those I work with or superintend; but on the whole things work smoothly, and I have no reason to complain.

How one longs for butter, milk, and fresh vegetables, and good bread. Biscuits (sometimes very musty), and the heaviest of doughey flat cakes or loaves, without any lubrication, are not a good substitute for home bread and butter. We get rice sometimes, which I enjoy, and compressed carrots and onions; sometimes dried beans. These, with tea, coffee, pepper, salt and lime juice, constitute our food and drink (and the tough ox we get for rations), but certainly I have rarely felt better. I now sleep inside a waggon, where I am at this present moment writing.

We are to have the Holy Communion next Sunday. How I am looking forward to it in the midst of all this work and anxiety. May our dear Lord make Himself very fully known to me in the breaking of bread, and may I be enabled to realise the blessedness of the Communion of the mystic Body of Christ, even His Holy Church, His saints on earth and in Paradise.

Please thank May and Flo a hundred times for their letters. It was so good of them to write. It is disappointing to think there are letters waiting in Natal to be brought on to me here, but stopped on account of our being thus cut off. How eagerly I shall look for the first convoy that is able to get up. I hope they will ere long muster troops sufficient at the Tugela to escort one.

I am hoping to hear that the Afghan War has been carried on successfully, and is now perhaps over, and that 'Barney' will have distinguished himself and get his majority.[6]

Give my father my kindest love, and thank him for all his great kindness and consideration; and also very much love to my sisters, and Skeff and Charley.

Abundance of love to the dear little mother and all our dear ones. Kiss our little pets for me very fondly.'

On the morning of the 7th, possibly just as Warren Wynne was writing home, another runner arrived, bearing the fullest account yet of the disaster. He added dramatically that John Dunn's road was 'buzzing with Zulu patrols',[7] and it was far too risky to attempt a return journey. It was clear to all that the noose was tightening around Eshowe. Wynne noted a nervousness amongst the soldiery.

¶ Sunday, February 9th – Divine service at 10am. No work to-day for the first time for some weeks now. Zulus observed to be collecting in the neighbourhood. Alarm given at 9pm; 5 or 6 shots fired by Buffs at a grey shirt hung up by some one in glacis to dry and forgotten.'

¶ February 11th, 12th, 13th – On the 11th two runners arrived from the Lower Tugela bearing a despatch from the General with what almost amounted to an order for Col Pearson to retire with about half his force to the Tugela, leaving the remainder to garrison the fort. At the Council of War of Commanding Officers and the Colonel's staff it was felt that the attempt to retire with 500 or 600 men would be very hazardous, seeing that the country between us and the Tugela is occupied (at least there is little doubt of it) by a large Zulu force, who would quickly become aware of our intention and endeavour to surround us in some position of disadvantage to us. It was, however, considered necessary to be prepared for performing what the General seemed to be bent upon – and secret arrangements were provisionally made. Three section of my Company were to accompany the Flying Column and the other section to remain here with one subaltern. The Colonel sent back a despatch to the General asking for further instructions.'

The despatch from Chelmsford indicated that Eshowe could expect nothing at all in the way of men or supplies for six weeks at the very least. Pearson's response was to send a detailed plan of retirement for the general's approval. If he was to retire from fort Eshowe, Colonel Pearson wanted explicit orders to that effect. Only then would he march out with the 99th, the Naval Brigade and the bulk of Wynne's sappers, taking no wheeled transport. This was to take place on the 16th, if Chelmsford consented. The messenger left the fort at nightfall on the 11th, slipping out into the shadows.

¶ Sunday, February 16th – Church parade at 10am. Wet afternoon; wet and stormy night. Anxiously looking out for further news from the General and the Lower Tugela. Fear the runners either thither or from thence to us have been intercepted and killed by the Zulus.'

This was indeed the case. The courier had been waylaid on the road, and killed. The plans he carried, of course, never reached Lord Chelmsford. No news came. Unwilling to make the decision to retire on his own authority, Pearson shrank from taking any initiative at all. The garrison settled into a routine of vigilance, short rations, sleeping fully clothed, and working on Wynne's fortifications. There was a programme of events – band concerts, swimming, edifying lectures and Bible study – all the things the Victorian army devised to keep the soldiers' minds off more traditional military pastimes such as gambling, quarrelling and drinking. There was nothing to drink – no ration rum or the rough Natal gin known as 'Squareface' or 'The Queen's Tears'. Life was harsh for underfed soldiers sleeping with belt and boots on, huddled under the wagons in pouring rain. Corporal F W Licence, of Wynne's company, was to write to his parents of 'fearful hard times of it in Eshowe'.[8] As a sapper, he was employed on the fort 'all day long, Sundays as well' while others had time for leisure. On the 18th, Captain Wynne was able to write a long letter home:-

¶ 'ESHOWE, 18th February 1879 – There is another 'runner' going to attempt the journey down to the Tugela (37 miles) to-night, so I will not lose the opportunity of sending a letter on the chance of its being posted and reaching you. The runners are faithful Kaffirs, they run great risks, for the Zulus are always on the look out to intercept them, and we have good reason to fear that the last who were sent down were taken and killed, for we have been left without news since the 11th inst, when a very important despatch was received from Lord Chelmsford to which a reply was sent off the same night. An answer ought to have arrived within three or at least four days, but none yet received.

Lord Chelmsford's despatch contained what almost amounted to an order that Colonel Pearson, leaving behind a garrison of 600 or 700 for this fort, should retreat, carrying nothing but arms, ammunition, and two days' rations on the person, without wagons or other conveyance, to the Tugela. The force would be about 500 men. It was a serious step and was considered by our Council of War here as very hazardous, seeing we should be dividing our forces and would probably meet the enemy in strong force in the bush along our line of retreat. However, we have been preparing if necessary to perform this, starting soon after midnight, going by a straight across country track, and doing the distance, about 30 miles, in one march. The General's reply has, however, not yet arrived, and I think it very probable he may look upon it as desirable to change his plan and leave us all here for the present, till reinforcements can be brought up, for we heard by the same despatch of the welcome arrival (or early expected arrival) at the Cape of two more regiments from England. There is no doubt the strength of the Zulus was under-rated, and too much stress was laid upon the belief in a split in their camp, and the peace party coming over to our side. If we go down to Tugela, I take three-fourths of my Company, leaving one officer here with the remainder. I fully believe God will mercifully protect us, and trust that He will bring me safely through. Then how joyfully I shall receive your letters which must now be awaiting me there. I fear the campaign is likely to be prolonged much beyond what was expected, though one never can tell in these wars against savages how soon they may collapse or how long resist.

We have hitherto gone on the principle of sparing their crops, so that they might not suffer from famine after peace was proclaimed. The principle seems good at first, but is not really merciful, since it enables them to prolong the war. It is a war of necessity, both expedient and just, but it is likely to be a rather disagreeable one.

Our work goes on here continuously. I have about 300 men daily working under me, and the natural disadvantages of the position are greatly being eliminated.

My 'Journal,' [ie the Diary] when you come to read it, will I fear be very dry, for I have no time to do more than keep a semi-official one. Up at 5am, and in bed at 8pm; I really am at work all day except during meals. We are on 'short rations' now, but for me these, though frugal and monotonous, are quite sufficient, so there is an advantage in being a rather small eater.

AFRICAN RUNNERS IN THE ZULU WAR

African messengers were in many ways the unsung heroes of the campaign. All despatches into and out of Fort Eshowe were carried by runners, slipping into and out of the fort under cover of darkness, or sprinting the final stretch to elude pursuit by Zulu patrols. These couriers were men in the service of prominent settlers in the frontier zone – the border agent Finney; Bishop Schreuder, or the 'White Zulu' John Dunn. Dunn recalled that there had been 'high reward offered if I could get anyone I could depend on to run despatches to the besieged'.[1] Two of his servants made the hazardous journey three times together. On the first trip the pair evaded the enemy; on the second they barely escaped an ambush. The last run, however, proved fatal. Ambushed once again, the man bearing the pack of letters was killed, and his companion forced to make his way back to the river while the Zulus scoured the bush. Lord Chelmsford had promised that the messengers would be amply repaid, and compensation paid to the families of anyone killed carrying out their mission. Dunn, however, noted bitterly that '...nothing ever came of it, beyond what I paid myself and a couple of sovereigns given by the Rev. Robertson. So much for the word of anyone representing the authority of a military government.'[2]

References

1) Cited in D F C Moodie, *The History of the Battles and Adventures of the British, the Boers and the Zulus &c in Southern Africa* Vol II, London, 1888, p.501–2.
2) Ibid, p.502.

The Zulus have made no attempt as yet to attack us. I fear they are too cunning, knowing that they would suffer severely, even if they tried to take the place by surprise. I am happy to say Colonel Pearson seems to be full of approval of my efforts and the result, and it will probably be of use to me hereafter if I am spared, having had this opportunity.

I think the plan of the campaign was a mistaken one, to march on the King's kraal or capital, along three or four lines, widely separated, and without chance of communication. It is also so difficult to get along in this country, where you have to carry everything in cumbersome ox-wagons, which delay your march and take up such length of road, 16 oxen to a wagon carrying only 4,000 lbs. Our Column was about $4^1/_2$ miles long, for 2,500 men. Whereas the Zulus, having no commissariat to look after, can attack in front, flanks, and rear, when and wherever they like. They also have a much larger supply of rifles and guns of all sorts than was supposed. Of course it is only a question of time, and they will be completely defeated, but it might have been done, I think, more quickly, and therefore with less cost. The worst of it is that whereas before their strength was under-rated, now, people are running into the opposite extreme and becoming over cautious.

All however is in God's hands, and night and day that thought comforts and sets my mind at rest. My thoughts are very frequently, even in the midst of much anxious and responsible work (for I have had the responsibility of very much since the defence of this place commenced) turned towards you and our precious children. I fear you may have been made very anxious about this time by the accounts which will have reached England of the disaster to the other Column. How I wish I could be with you, if only for an hour, to speak words of hope and encouragement. I do morning and night pray that these may be supplied to you by Him who can speak to the inmost soul.

I wish I could have found time to write to Mother, Flo, and May, or either of them, as I intended doing this afternoon, but one of my subalterns was most anxious to ride out to a neighbouring hill, and I could not refuse him, so had to superintend some work of his on the fort. My love in abundance to all the dear ones everywhere.'

The Zulus did not leave the garrison alone. Numbers of warriors were visible most of the time, and nobody doubted that, in the Inyezane forest, 'a savage host, estimated at thirty thousand',[9] was ready to strike at any British force that moved in the open. Outpost duty was a hazardous enterprise. A scratch force of thirty or so mounted infantrymen was raised, using some of the officers' horses, together with some left behind by Major Barrow owing to sickness. There were four posts of vedettes, each of three men at a time, about a mile from the camp.

As a security arrangement, this plan proved inadequate. Current theory suggested that whole battalions or cavalry regiments should be used in a deep net of outposts – reserves, supports, piquets, 'Cossack posts' and, finally, single or double vedettes placed some 2,000 yards from the main body, and ideally twice that distance. Pearson did not have the manpower to follow this system; but he ought to have been able to find more than twelve men for his 'eyes and ears'. As it was, Zulu bands waited in the brush to deliver ragged volleys at the vedettes as they arrived at their stations at sunrise. Private Kent was killed while riding ahead of his comrades, who were forced to watch as half a dozen Zulus shot his horse and assegaied the helpless man before running off with his Martini-Henry and ammunition. Private Carsons of the 99th barely escaped the same fate on a later occasion, spurring his horse into a gallop despite gunshot wounds so serious that he had to be invalided out of the army. After this, a whole company was used to clear the ground every morning.

¶ 'February 18th – Lecture by Rev Mr Robinson, on History of Zululand at 5.30.'

¶ 'February 20th – At 5.15pm, a second lecture from Rev Mr Robertson on History of Zululand. We are still absolutely cut off from the world, no news since the 11th.'

¶ 'February 21st – A small raid made in a northerly direction, two miles from the fort, none of the enemy seen; distant firing heard about 11am in the direction of Fort Buckingham.'[10]

The raids by the mounted men, on the 21st and the following day, though small operations, were a sign that the British were beginning to regain the initiative.

¶ 'ESHOWE, Sunday, 23rd February 1879 – Another day of rest – not only a Sunday – but, what I have not had lately, a Sunday without obligation to work, and how acceptable it is I cannot fully describe. It comes with such unusual peace, being able to feel that, though not absolutely freed from the cares and responsibilities of my work, I can give up my thoughts to heavenly things – to a calm consideration of God's great goodness, and mercy, and love, and to enjoyment of communion with Him, through Jesus our dear Lord. That I can also allow my mind unreservedly to turn to those heavenly-earthly reflections which are concentrated upon our dear home.

To-day is a wet, wet Sunday, and we were unable to have service this morning. I have just been reading the Psalms for this morning, very beautiful they are. I find so much that is applicable and full of comfort and encouragement in the Psalms now beyond what I ever did before. I have unfortunately no Table of the Lessons,[11] so am unable to read the same as you have at home; and we only have a portion of the Service at Church parades. It is now exactly 1.38pm with us, and therefore as near as possible 11.30am with you. I am thinking of you reading the same Psalms, either in Church (dear All Saints) or in the house, if baby keeps you in. Last night between 11 and 1 we had a terrific thunderstorm. I never heard such angry thunder. The rain came down in buckets full, and I was glad we had just finished the drainage of the ditch round the fort. The main drain which carries off the water from the lowest point, and which was eleven feet under ground was, however, damaged in one part by the rush of water through it. The tarpaulin over my waggon kept me dry, with the exception of one tiny place. I fear the men fared worse a good deal. I am going to commence as soon as possible to make them huts of wattle and clay, with plastered roofs – a kind of hurdle work. All the defences of this place are now completed, I may say, though I intend improving them in places if we remain here.

We are still without an atom of news – have heard nothing since the 11th instant, and I may say next to nothing except of the disaster of the 22nd January, since we left the Tugela five weeks ago. One feels entirely cut off and exiled. My work has been incessant from 5am till 8pm ever since we arrived here, this day month, and most thankful I am to our Heavenly Father that He has prospered me so in my health to enable me to do what was required of me with fair success.

The Zulus show no signs of an intention of attacking us here. It is a pity they do not come, for the result would probably influence the war very much in the way of shortening it. We are full of eager curiosity to learn what they are meditating. Two days ago we heard distant firing as of artillery, about twenty miles off, and have been wondering if an engagement has taken place. The General has not, so far as we know, reiterated the order (of which I told you in my letter of the 18th) for half our garrison to retire to the Tugela. I have been fearing that for the last week and for some days to come you may be going through a time of anxiety through the arrival in England by telegram of vague news, about the disaster to the 24th Regiment at Isandhlwana, and the loss of so many officers – long before you get my letter telling you of our successful engagement at Inyezane, and of my being attached to a column in a different part of Zululand from that which suffered. However, I hope the telegram may have been explicit, and so give no ground for alarm.

The climate up here is a very pure and healthy one. We have warm sunny days and cool nights, with heavy rains about twice a week. Yesterday the thermometer went up to 89° in the shade, otherwise 79° was the average for the week, and at 6am only 64°. To-day, after the rain, it is, at the present moment, only 65°. I am now inclined to think Maritzburg[12] will be our quarters, and, on the whole, believe it would suit us best. I am like a schoolboy in looking forward to that day of our meeting. It will be a honeymoon, and no mistake! What a long three months it has seemed since that sudden and unpleasant telegram arrived at Eastbourne.

I do not know whether it is worth my trying to give you a description of this Fort. By-and-by, when there is no fear of my letters not going forward by the mail, I will make a drawing of it and the hill features round it for you. There is about 500 yards length of parapet all round, and a ditch 7ft. deep, and, in some places 11ft., in others 10ft. wide. The men on the parapets are at present protected in rear from fire coming across the fort from the opposite side, by waggons drawn in a line in rear of the parapets. On the waggons are sacks of earth, etc., and across the waggons are stretched tarpaulins tied to upright posts, so that the men have shelter under them at night and in wet weather. These I am going to replace by degrees by huts of wattle or hurdle work and clay. Then they are also protected from fire on the right or left by what are called traverses,[13] made either of piles of sacks of earth, or grass sods built in courses, or wattled clay walls placed at intervals along the parapet. So they ought to be safe enough, no matter how strong the force which attacks them.

My waggon is drawn up just inside the parapet, on the lower side of the fort. I am better off than most (although some officers have tents) my waggon having a roof made of a bamboo arch, covered with tarpaulin, and inside I have my camp bedstead, and a biscuit packing case for table and wardrobe. My waterproof bucket serves for washstand, basin, and all. I sleep in my clothes, but have lately left off boots and patrol jacket. The loaded revolver is always handy, but has not been used as yet, nor, indeed, do I wish it to be, for I am sure I have no desire to take the life of one of these fellows, unless in duty bound. Lieut. Main, of ours, and I grub together, ie join rations, but we all four, ie Courtney and Willock as well, sit at one table for meals under a pleasant shady tree, which we monopolized from the first. There we chew the generally very tough, much stewed ox, with, as a rule, about a tablespoon of preserved carrots, sometimes some large haricot beans. These, and either biscuit, or a kind of 'fadge',[14] manufactured by my servant, out of Boer's meal, a sort of oatmeal, is our daily food at breakfast, lunch, and dinner; in fact, every meal the same, except that we have coffee at breakfast and tea at dinner. I really do not mind it, but most fellows get very tired of it, and complain of insufficiency. Yesterday, there was a sale of the private effects found in the waggons left behind by the Mounted Volunteers who came with us, but returned to Natal when the news of the disaster reached us, on the 28th January. The following is a sample of the prices which articles fetched. The auction was open to both officers and men. One ham (12-lbs.) £6.5s. Tins of condensed milk, 26s. each. Small tin of cocoa, 11s 6d. Bottle of curry powder (small), 23s. Boxes of matches (1/2d boxes), 6s per dozen. I need scarcely tell you that this child bought nothing on this occasion.

We have been lately making some raids into the neighbourhood to burn kraals (*small settlements*) and bring in mealies (*maize*). There is to be one to-morrow. It will be wet work, the rain has continued all day, it is now (7pm) raining hard. However, the Kaffir or Zulu is always easy to tackle in wet weather, which he dislikes very much, and no wonder, considering his limited attire. They are sending down another runner to-night by a different track, in the hope of his getting down to Natal safely, which they fear has not been the case with, at least, two of the former ones. I have sent you letters dated the 22nd and 28th ultimo, the 4th and 18th inst., and, I think, also the 2nd inst.[15] It remains to be seen whether they will reach you. Meanwhile it is trying to me to have had but two letters from you in nearly three months – the latest dated December 12th.

I am making a survey of the neighbourhood of this place, and I was contouring yesterday and the day before. I was glad to be at the old work again,[16] and pleasant memories of past days kept crowding upon me. Of various expeditions (and in spite of the train work I should be glad to be at them again), and my returns home often an hour or so earlier than I had told you, and the happy greetings from you and the 'chicks'; or the jolly evenings at the dear little mother's[17] at Guildford.

Well, well! there's a good time coming, and when it comes we shall know how to enjoy it, and bless God for it. I never was so full of feelings of thankfulness to Him as I nowam for all the benefits He has bestowed upon me, of which I was so unworthy. May He ever bless you and give you all help and encouragement.'

¶ 'Ash Wednesday [18] – But no note of the Church fast here. Nor have I had so much as five minutes since I rose at 5 o'clock to give my thoughts to what should be so solemn a season – and much I wish it were otherwise, for I greatly need it – to try and examine my heart and lay open by the help of the Holy Spirit and His Word its great sinfulness, its particular faults and shortcomings. I must endeavour this Lenten season to gain some time daily for serious reflection and self-examination, and may God bless it with profit to my soul, to the glory of His grace.

I must leave off as it is nearly bedtime, 8pm (or 6pm with you). It is funny to think that I should be going to bed before our baby boy!

What an eloquent peaceful happy text is that 'Be ye therefore followers of God as dear children; and walk in love; as Christ also hath loved us, and hath given Himself for us as an offering and a sacrifice to God for a sweet smelling savour.' May we and ours, and especially our little ones always be His 'dear children' and walk in love.'

Food is a constant theme in Wynne's letters. The common soldier was used to a monotonous diet of miserably prepared beef and bread. However, if the food was bad, it usually came in large quantities, and was augmented by jams, pickles and preserved vegetables from the regimental canteen. At Eshowe officers and men alike shared government rations – though, since the letters home from the Other Ranks do not mention any vegetables, these may have been a 'perk' reserved for the holders of Her Majesty's Commission. Wolseley had this to say on the matter:

¶ 'Messing is always a difficult matter, for English officers will carry their preconceived notions of comfort into the field with them. They must learn to live as much like the men as possible – any officer who cannot make up his mind to live upon the same fare as his men, had better remain at home with his mother.'[19]

Shortening rations meant that daily issue was now 6 oz biscuit, 6 oz flour, $^1/_3$oz tea, $^1/_2$ oz coffee, $^1/_2$ oz sugar, and a piece of beef supposedly of $1^1/_4$ lbs, reported by Corporal Licence as 'The oxen that drew our waggons up, and it was so tough that we have had to throw it away after it was cooked.'[20] He went on to say that 'the only thing that we could eat was the soup and biscuits if we had any left, not very often.' Another soldier pronounced the meat 'trek oxen, flesh hard as india-rubber, and useless.'[21] Whenever possible, forage parties scoured the hills for mealie patches, roasting the cobs of maize or, like Wynne's servant, grinding them to porridge meal.

NOTES

1) Major General Sir Garnet Wolseley, *The Soldier's Pocket-Book for Field Service* (3rd edition, London, 1874) pp 196–200.
2) *The Official Narrative* (p. 54) states that 1,000 oxen were sent, and that 900 of them were seized by the Zulus.
3) Deo Volente - 'God Willing'
4) Arthur was Wynne's eldest son, born to his first wife.
5) The reference to a letter of 12th January is a mistake: Wynne refers to that of December 12th.
6) The Second Afghan War appeared to be close to a successful conclusion at the end of 1878 – but hostilities broke out again the following September, and it was to be 1881 before the last British forces left Afghanistan. 'Barney' was Wynne's brother Arthur.
7) Morris, op cit p. 430
8) Emery, op cit p. 213
9) Ibid, p. 211
10) Fort Buckingham was a minor earthwork a few miles east of the Middle Drift. It was built in 1861 and abandoned in 1868, though it may have served as an outpost station in the Zulu War. I have found no record of any action there or thereabouts on February 21st.
11) A daily lectionary consisting of prescribed readings from the Old and New Testaments, and the Psalms.
12) A shortened form of Pietermaritzburg.
13) Fourteen traverses in all.
14) 'Fudge' in modern parlance.
15) If Wynne wrote a letter home on 2nd February, Lucy never received it.
16) This refers to Wynne's peacetime duties for the Ordnance Survey in England.
17) My assumption is that this was Lucy's mother.
18) 26th February.
19) Wolseley, op cit p. 13
20) Emery, op cit p. 213
21) Staff Sergeant Beatson, 99th Regiment; Emery, op cit p. 210

WORKING PARTIES AT ESHOWE, 29th January – 28th February

In his Diary, Wynne kept a tally of workmen for each day of construction. In tabular form it shows the following scale of labour:-

Date	Royal Engineers	Natal Native Pioneers	Infantry & Naval Brigade	Notes
January				
29	61	40	160	
30	65	50	230	'For 7 $\frac{1}{2}$ hours'
31	60	40	200	'Working hours 6 to 8, 9 to 12, 1.30 to 5'
February				
1				No record
2	(Planned rest day)			'Worked 1.30 to 4.30'
3	50	40	150	6–8, 9.30–12, 1.30–4.30
4	55	40	200	'Working hours as yesterday'
5	50	40	130	ditto
6–8				No record
9				Rest Day
10	60	45	140	'Working hours as usual'
11–13	60	45	80	ditto
14	55	45	145	
15	60	50	120	
16				Rest Day
17				No record
18–20				'Same working party as usual, and same hours'
21	59	50	approx 150	Varied hours for each infantry unit
22	60	no record approx 125		ditto
23				Rest Day
24	62 (5 hrs) no record approx 100 (2.5 hrs each)			
25	50	40	approx 75	
26	60 (7.5 hrs)	45 (4.5 hrs)	80 (7.5 hrs)	
27	59 (7.5 hrs)	48 (4.5 hrs)	70 (7.5 hrs)	
28	58 (6.5 hrs)	45 (5.5 hrs)	70	
Total Man-Hours worked				
	10,385	6,863.5	19,662.5	
Grand total	36,910.5 total			

(= Estimates, assuming work done on half of the 'no record' days)

Chapter Nine: Eshowe III - The Fort

Eshowe had been intended as an entrenched supply depot for a small garrison to hold. In the last days of January it had become a firebase, a hastily built-up breastwork expecting the onslaught of 20,000 Zulus. As January folded over into February, and no assault came, Eshowe grew from a mere fieldwork into a fortress. The site was never intended for a fort. Chosen because of its permanent buildings by men who knew it only as a point on a map, the Norwegian mission had few of the features of a good position. It was built on a fairly level piece of ground at the head of a valley that ran towards the south-east; thus the highest point of Fort Eshowe was at the north-west angle. On viewing the mission for the first time, Colonel Pearson made this observation to Lord Chelmsford:

¶ '....from a military view... it is the ugliest bit of ground for a camp or a defensible post I have seen. However the buildings... which have all been left – are so good for stores that it would be a pity to abandon it for another site.' [1]

The key problem with Eshowe was that it was overlooked by hills on three sides at a distance of a few hundred yards – within easy rifle range for Zulu snipers. Since it was impossible to build the parapets to a height where this serious drawback could be resolved, Wynne had placed defensive traverses to protect the garrison from fire from the flanks and rear. The fort was an irregular hexagon, some 150 yards on the longer east-west axis, and roughly 50 wide. With ditch, parapets and traverses in place, and the outlying buildings properly demolished, Eshowe was defensible. Captain Wynne's efforts were henceforth devoted to improving not only the details of the fortifications, but the quality of the living conditions:-

¶ 'January 29th – South face completely revetted, parapet nearly finished. East face (containing salient)[2] revetting done chiefly by Naval Brigade, for want of sufficient RE. Work indifferent – and the profiles having been spoilt, the parapet made too thin. North and west faces still very incomplete. (The north face was intended to have a parapet from 8'6' to 7'). The stockade at south-east angle was proceeded with, being formed between tall gum trees about 24' girth for uprights, with horizontal timbers between supporting rows of sand bags. It is intended to make a gallery for a double tier of musketry firing down valley to south-east, at present thickly wooded, but being gradually cleared.'

The stockade was built to provide an upper firing platform – sometimes known as a 'cavalier' – to reinforce the defences on the low-lying south-east angle. As a log structure, the stockade took up considerably less space inside the crowded fort than would an earthwork.

¶ 'January 30th – An alarm at 1.30pm caused inconvenient stoppage of work and some rough handling of parapets.

Weather hot. Examined at 5.30am, a better place for cattle laager, by which the masking of fire of the present one might be avoided. The spot containing least disadvantages seemed to be the kloof running down from within 30 yards of the west face. This was approved by Col. Pearson, and I set the Natal Pioneers to clear away the brush-wood and timber stumps still left.'

¶ 'January 31st – Hurdle revetment finished round fort, but portion of east faces badly done was now revetted, also a portion of west face which had given away. Excavation of ditches of west, north and east faces continued; also of stockade. Native Pioneers continued grubbing up stumps, &c, in kloof on west side, and commenced sinking a well close to ditch of west face, it being contemplated to throw out a lunette[3] in front of that face to flank the laager.

Camp beginning to be fouled through close occupation by human beings and horses. Improved scavenging arrangements made; a place made in upper part of north face for picketing the horses.[4] Remounted RA and RN guns and Gatlings. One 7 pr RA at north-west and one at south-west angle. Two 7 pr RN (at special request both together) at north-east angle, and the Gatling on the south face, 40 yards from stockade.

Constructed a main drain with outlet into ditch through east face near salient. Constructed a gateway and barriers in west face. Barriers simply of double planking sliding up and down between pairs of posts on either side, with loopholes cut in the upper planks.

¶ 'February 1st – Wet all night and early morning. From 6 to 8 all hands at work improving the drainage of the camp. Drain made in stockade.

Reconnoitred ground within a mile of south side of camp.

Continued deepening ditches, felling timber and clearing brushwood, sinking well to 12 feet. Arranged for formation of laager in kloof below west face, in a trapezoidal form, with the longest parallel side nearest to, and parallel with, the west face. Loophole gallery in church reconstructed.[5] A look-out place made in church tower. The waggon traverses, ie, waggons with sacks of earth piled on them for protection from raking and from reverse fire, proceeded with. As sacks of provisions are emptied by the Commissariat they are sent to the RE store and issued again by us for the purpose. Biscuit boxes, in like manner, are ordered to be sent to us to be broken up and used for small planking. Our work is seriously hindered for want of squared timber, planking timber in the rough – that is of any good length and straight, and specially for want of spikes and nails, rope and lashings.'

¶ 'Sunday, February 2nd – Rained all night. Camp in a fearful state of mud and greasy clay. Church parade postponed to tomorrow morning on account of wet. Native Pioneers employed deepening ditch near north-east angle. All tools handed over to RE to form a general park. A small re-issue made per company for camp requirements. Commenced sinking shaft for communication with proposed caponier, south ditch.'

The caponier was an extremely unusual and ambitious addition to the fort. This device of the fortress engineer was an enclosed corridor cut directly across the ditch, with firing ports cut into it in order to rake an enemy storming party as they tried to cross the moat. The defenders of the caponier would enter via a narrow portal cut through the inner parapet, and it was this 'communication' that was Wynne's first step.

¶ 'February 3rd – Church parade at 8.45am. Constructing flanks for laager, to be occupied by 15 men each, who could fall back through a sallyport in west face.[6] Caponier communication continued, also timbers brought from kloof, half a mile off, and shaped for construction of caponier. Sallyport in west face commenced. Felling and clearing continued, also deepening of ditches and spreading surplus earth over glacis. Spouting made and fixed under eaves of church roof to catch rain in waggon tank below. Traverses for guns and parapets constructed.

Issued to each company for camp purposes:- 10 picks, 10 shovels, 6 billhooks, 3 hand axes,1 felling axe.'

February 4th witnessed the beginning of several new projects. Wynne added a drawbridge over the ditch at the newly built west gate, a small bridge at the north-east where the drainage ran off, and minor works to complement the caponier.

¶ 'February 4th – Got a small supply of coals and set an RE smith to work. Deepening ditches, felling timber in kloof. Continued sallyport, west face; commenced drawbridge, main entrance, west face; continued flanks for laager and communications. Commenced two short indents[7] in parapet north face, to flank ditches on either side of re-entering angle.[8] Burning and cleaning pieces of cover on hill to east of work, also bush in valley to south-east. Commenced a foot bridge at 'Water-gate',[9] north-east angle. Well sunk 20ft – no very good result as yet.'

¶ 'February 5th – Work of yesterday continued. Constructed a blindage[10] for RA gun, south-west angle; posts 8' or 9' diam., and sandbags.'

¶ 'February 6th – Blindages made for gun RA at north-west angle and Gatling on south face; also a traverse made for parapet, south face, out of piles of ox waggon yokes. Continued other work as before detailed.'

¶ 'February 7th – Commenced shallow trous de loup,[11] 3ft square and 2ft deep, as obstacles, about 25 yards from east ditches; cut down glacis in several places; constructed blindage for naval guns. Commenced a small magazine for loose powder left behind in flasks by Native Contingent, and which we placed in empty M H ammunition boxes;[12] built it against vestry wall of church of rough timber 3' to 4' diam. for posts and framing, roof and sides boarded with biscuit boxes then plastered 1' with clay and cowdung, over which a covering of sheets of corrugated iron which happened to be spare. Another rendering of clay and cowdung, and all round both sides and over roof sandbags.

Filled in old bank and trench near foot of north glacis, and did other work to prevent the enemy obtaining cover in the vicinity of the fort – about 60 Infantry employed in this. Commenced a triangulation[13] of neighbourhood of fort for future survey.'

Wynne's care and concern in building the powder magazine is

understandable. The explosion of a magazine had proved disastrous in more than one well-known instance, and the fact that the Zulus owned no artillery did not mean that the powder was safe from accident or freak effects of musketry.

There was no entry in the journal for February 8th; the 9th was a Sunday, and a welcome day of rest.

¶ 'February 10th – Commenced work at 5am and was at it without intermission, excepting meals, till 6pm. Observed angles for triangulation.

Continued trous de loup, sallyport and caponier; commenced a new battery at east salient for one naval gun, which it was decided to separate from the other at north-east angle. Water gate drawbridge completed. Filling in hollows and clearing cover outside fort. Commenced gate for closing sallyport; gate slides up and down between two pairs of posts. Completed observation of angles for triangulation.'

¶ 'February 11th, 12th, 13th – Cutting drain 11' deep at counterscarp,[14] and running through stockade and glacis, from bottom of ditch 30 yards towards south stream (not connected with water supply). This was found necessary to drain ditches of fort. Plastering thatched roof of building in fort with clay and cowdung. Paving roadway main gate with bricks; 11th, finished magazine. Sack traverses continued; also naval gun battery at east salient. Re-adjusting sandbag protection to windows in hospital (church).'

The range markers consisted of white stones laid out at set distances. Captain MacGregor wrote that 'Wynne has given us no end of ranges in all directions, and really I fear there is no hope of an attack now'. Although the Martini-Henry was sighted to 1,400 yards, experienced officers did not expect their men to engage in effective fire at much over 700. Soldiers tended to forget to adjust range sights in the excitement of firing, a dangerous vice in face of the speed of a Zulu attack, and range markers enabled company officers and NCOs to call out precise distances on cue.

¶ 'February 13th – I laid down on the ground ranges from 300 to 700 yards round fort.'

¶ 'February 14th – Rain came on at noon and lasted all the afternoon. Commenced cutting down glacis of west face and filling in flanks and communications to protect laager, Col. Pearson having decided that he could not be sure of these flanks being held for any time if the enemy were close at hand. I arranged to use the sallyport, west face, for the communication with a new caponier[15] to be constructed to flank west ditch and main entrances. This was therefore commenced. Having by means of posts marked on the ground opposite the fort several musketry ranges from 300 to 700 yards, and laid these points down on a scale 1/4800, I handed this in to Col.Pearson, who approved, and gave orders for it to be copied by Officers commanding companies and turned to account by a study of the ground.

Continued plastering roof; commenced wire entanglements[16] opposite north-east angle; continued drain south-east angle and felling timber in kloof.'

¶ 'February 15th – Wet morning; no work 6 to 8. Continued same work as yesterday. Surveyed fort.'

Warren Wynne next turned his considerable attention to one of the mission buildings that had found itself at the northernmost point of the parapet. This was to become a block-house to guard the water gate:-

¶ 'February 17th – Determined to improve the defence of north-east angle – where small loop-holed brick house and 'Water Gate' are situated, and which is undoubtedly weak – by re-roofing the house so as to slope to the front and by filling in half the blindage and constructing loopholes between the sandbags to obtain effective musketry fire down the glacis opposite this angle. The battery now has but one naval gun.[17] Also to make a skew traverse[18] with banquette behind it on south face about 15 yards below hospital, high enough to fire over men on parapet and also to screen men on upper part of this face from raking fire from distant hill to south-east. The heavy rains have made the fort, through which there is so much traffic (about 1,500 men and about a dozen horses) in a dreadful state of mud. Weather so showery that only a few RE and Native Pioneer could be employed, but no infantry.'

¶ 'February 18th – Arranged alterations in small brick building, so as to have fire from three sides: from west side to flank north glacis and re-entering angle ditch with about four rifles. Water Gate communication to be flanked by three rifles from north side, and east salient and glacis to be flanked by five rifles from east side. The building, which was very slight and insecure, to be unroofed, strengthened by stout posts, 9' above the ground, framed together. Brickwork to be added as in sketch[19] on west side, and sod revetment on north and east sides. This arrangement (in place of that which I thought of yesterday) I commenced to-day. Continued caponier west ditch; felling timber in kloof; repairing main drain south-east, which had been spoiled at mouth by floods before completion; cutting drains in ditch and repairing a piece of escarp below stockade which had been undermined by water in ditch. Blocking up windows by split logs to render them bullet proof, replacing cumbrous earth sacks; cutting away west glacis; plastering roof; clearing cover round fort.'

¶ 'February 19th – Continued work at north-east angle on small brick building; finished west caponier; commenced high traverse in front of north door of hospital; timber framing with clay between wattling, 11 feet high, 2'3' at bottom, with a small batter[20] on one side; finished blocking up windows in hospital; continued repairs of main drain; clearing cover, cutting away west glacis; commenced a large field oven[21] for RE; a raid made today and a waggon load of mealies brought in. I rode out with Col. Pearson and Staff to Stony hill and Conical hill; and towards Umlalazi valley in the afternoon.'

¶ 'February 20th – Continued work on flanking building at Water Gate and loopholed the gallery beside (NE) naval gun. A party finishing steps down to communication with caponier west ditch; continued blocking up hospital windows for bullet proofs; strengthened west door of hospital for bullet proof; half finished wattled traverse in front of north door of hospital (vestry room). Commenced a similar one on south face oblique to parapet, affording fire from three rifles (half-way between caponier and east end of hospital); continued large oven for the RE, also plastering thatched roof of Commissariat stores; felling timber in kloof by Native Pioneers; party with mule wagons employed fetching bricks and stones from demolished buildings on south hill; continued cutting down west glacis. I commenced contouring[22] the ground immediately surrounding the fort; Willock assisted.'

The survey work involved in tracing the contour lines around the fort must have been a reminder of peace time duties in the midst of extending the fort. By this time most of the work being done was finishing touches of various kinds. One new project, which reflected the increasing permanence of the Eshowe garrison, was the plan for wattle huts to replace the cramped and unhealthy sleeping arrangements under the wagons. Wynne does not elaborate on this, and the question as to where all these were to be placed remains unanswered:-

¶ 'February 21st – Repairs to main gate bridge completed; Water Gate masonry flanks, &c, nearly finished, also traverse in front of vestry door; wattled traverse south face, plastering of roofs, cutting down west glacis, steps for communication with caponier, felling timber, and cutting brushwood for hutting, &c, continued. An armed covering party always accompanies the Natal Pioneers while employed in this last work. Filling in deep pits in south glacis 70 yards from parapet; tripod[23] for slaughtered cattle put up for Commissariat on open space in front of north-west angle; large oven for RE completed; continued contouring around the neighbourhood of Fort.'

¶ 'February 22nd – Continued felling timber in far kloof; finished felling and clearing off wood in valley to south-east; carted stone from site of buildings on east hill; continued and nearly completed work at Water Gate; perfected drainage of West and East ditches; continued plastering thatched roofs; cutting down west glacis. A party of 6 RE has been permanently employed of late sharpening and repairing tools, helving axes, shovels, &c. Commenced making hurdles for huts; continued wattled traverse south face. I spent the greater part of the day contouring the ground round fort. Several Zulus seen by the party sent out to cut timber, two killed.'

On the 23rd the vulnerability of new earthworks to the elements was once again made obvious. Permanent earthen fortifications were held in place by sowing grass and planting saplings, whose roots would bind into the soil; the trees could, of course, be cut down when an attack was threatened. Even so, the upkeep of an earthwork demanded constant efforts:-

¶ 'February 23rd – Severe thunderstorm between eleven o'clock last night and one this morning. Rain fell in torrents; 15 paces length of the outfall of the drain from the ditch, opposite the stockade, damaged. The earth had not been filled in sufficiently over the drain and, therefore, the water collected in the hollow and washed the earth away. Rain fell more or less heavily all day.'

¶ 'February 24th – Heavy rain at night. Wet from 6 to 8am, which prevented work. A raid made at 9am to bring in mealies; kraal burnt, 200 Zulus seen.

Commenced putting up lightning conductors on church (hospital), macadamising and paving road outside main gate; continued traverse south face; hurdle making; Water Gate flank and masonry traverse; improving drainage; bringing over stone and brick from sites of houses south and east hills; filling in pits south glacis. Went with Mr Robertson three-quarters of a mile to westward to search for stone and brushwood in kloof. Wet evening and rain at night.'

The process of 'macadamising' involved the laying of small pieces of broken stone, ideally 'about the size of a hen's egg', according to Wolseley,[24] levelling the surface with stone hammers, then repeating the process:-

¶ 'February 25th – Misty morning and showers. Paving Water Gate entrance, making road from main gate, fetching stones and bricks from sites of houses; continued south traverse; repaired drain in glacis at stockade; repaired church roof which leaks; commenced the wattled huts south-east of fort; preparing timber, filling in pits, south glacis.'

¶ 'February 26th – Fine day. Laid out site and commenced construction of first block of huts near stockade, south-east angle; continued paving and macadamising roadway and main and water-gate entrances; traversed banquette, south face; large main drain in glacis, south-east angle; felling timber and cutting brushwood in kloof three quarters of a mile north-west of fort (Natal Pioneers). Stone and bricks carted from east hill; stable,north ditch; lightning conductor to church; improving scaffolding for 'look out man', church tower. A foraging party sent out today for mealies.'

¶ 'February 27th – Finished traverse, south face; continued paving and macadamising roadway through fort; finished main drain, south-east angle; stone carted from east hill; continued preparing stable[25] in north ditch by widening it and making floor; continued huts in south-east part of fort. A foraging party sent out to-day. I walked to Stony Hill and other stations to take further trigonometrical observations with sextant. Thunderstorm at night.'

¶ 'February 28th – Wet 6 to 8. Commenced cutting[26] sods for revetments of parapets of which the hurdle work has given way in places. It is proposed to replace it throughout. Continued paving road; commenced a second traverse (sod revetted) south face; continued carting stone from east hill; stable, north ditch; huts, south-east of fort. Natal Pioneers preparing *dager* (clay and cowdung) for roof and floors of huts in morning, felling timber in the afternoon, filling in pits, south glacis. Received orders for RE to join an expedition leaving the fort at 2am tomorrow, to attack a Military Kraal, 6 miles distant.'

By the end of February, the fort was effectively complete. The diary entries, though hardly the most invigorating pieces of literature, provide the valuable details of the field engineer at work. Through a myriad of construction projects Wynne developed a simple earth redoubt into a sophisticated field fortification with a number of elaborate features. Realistically, it is questionable whether caponiers and lunettes would have made much difference in beating off a Zulu assault, but that was hardly the point. Wynne had been an engineer for almost seventeen years, and he was doing his duty to the best of his ability.

NOTES

1) Cited in the Hon Gerald French, *Lord Chelmsford and the Zulu War*, (London 1939).
2) A salient is an angle of the fort extending out towards the enemy position.
3) A triangular work, usually extending into or beyond the glacis.
4) The horses were picketed in the ditch under the north wall.
5) This had probably been damaged in the fire of January 28th.
6) A sallyport is a tunnel or gate allowing the garrison to 'sally forth' at will.
7) The indents served to give flanking fire without making serious changes in the outlay of the work.
8) The re-entrant is the opposite of the salient – an angle facing inward.
9) The watergate survives to the present day – *vide* Laband and Thompson, op cit p. 47.
10) A blindage was an armoured shield for an artillery piece.
11) Literally, 'wolf holes':- pits with sharpened stakes at the bottom.
12) 'MH' refers to the Martini-Henry rifle.
13) A trigonometric calculation for locating a position by means of bearings from two fixed points at a set distance apart.
14) The cutting still exists at the site of Fort Eshowe.
15) The caponier would have matched that on the south face; no trace remains.
16) This was not barbed wire, but strong iron wire stretched in a web between posts to impede attackers.
17) It was, as we know, built for two.
18) A skew traverse was built diagonally rather than at 90° to the parapet.
19) No sketch, regrettably, remains.
20) A wall built with one side sloped to be narrower at the top than at the base.
21) It is unclear whether the oven was intended as a field bakery or as a brick kiln – probably the former.
22) Contouring was the procedure of measuring heights and tracing the lines of the contours for survey purposes.
23) Fresh killed meat would be hung for several hours before cooking, if possible.
24) Cited in Sir Garnet Wolseley, op cit, p. 127.
25) The stable was a development of the picketing place created in the north ditch.
26) Sod revetments were likely to prove longer lasting than wattle hurdle work.

Chapter Ten: Dabulamanzi's Kraals - A Raid by Moonlight

Eshowe had been invested for a month. There had been no contact with the outside world for more than two weeks. The fort was solidly built, and no serious attack had been mounted by the Zulus. The garrison was convinced that relief must come, and that Lord Chelmsford was poised to strike north from Natal with a new expeditionary force. If Colonel Pearson's men could not break out of their blockade, they could at least cause as many problems for Cetshwayo as possible. The timorous quality of the first weeks of the siege was abating, and there was an air of confidence at Fort Eshowe. No 1 Column had already mounted some minor raids against the Zulus in the surrounding countryside; on the early morning of March 1st, Captain Wynne accompanied the largest raiding party yet.

¶ '28th February – I was going to indulge in a short chat with you for half an hour or so to-day, but find my time cut short by orders and preparations for an expedition which we are to make to-morrow to attack a military 'kraal' about six miles from here. We leave at 2am, and hope to be back for breakfast. I must wait till our return to give an account of it, though very likely it will prove insignificant.'

Wynne recorded the events of the night in his Diary. In contrast to the dry prose of recent entries, the journal suggests the excitement he felt after a successful turn of dishing it out to the foe who had kept the force bottled up for so long:-

¶ 'March 1st – Paraded the Company at 2am and formed up on a road to north-west of fort in front of Columns, which consisted of 30 Mounted Infantry, 2nd Company RE, 1 gun RA, 4 Companies Buffs, Natal Native Pioneers (some as stretcher bearers), 1 Company 99th. We groped our way in the dark, passing close by thick bush a great part of the way, in a westerly direction, towards Enigwakain, the military Kraal of which Dabulamanzi,[1] brother to Cetshwayo, is commander. The distance was something over six miles. When within three-quarters of a mile of the Kraal, it being about 4.30am and nearly light, some of the Zulu outposts observed us. The Mounted Infantry were just too late in trying to cut them off. The RE were thrown out as skirmishers to the right front of the Column, facing a kloof, where the Zulus had appeared to run. The bush having been examined without result the column advanced, the RE being sent in skirmishing order to the left front, over a hill commanding the Kraal. Having gained this we passed down a deep kloof, with thick bush and sides, sloping 25°, which we examined and passed round, and then advanced through mealie fields to a position about 800 yards from the Kraal and 200 yards from the head of the Column. We saw about 50 Zulus to our left front making for the Kraal and would have fired upon them, though at long range, but that two or three had red coats[2] and there seemed to be two stretchers carried by them. This made us pause, thinking that by chance the Native Pioneers had found their way there. Meanwhile the inmates of the Kraal, who had evidently been taken by surprise, were seen streaming out and up the hill sides to their right rear, driving off cattle. The Mounted Infantry went forward and set fire to the Kraal, after a shell had been fired into it. The gun (7 pr) was then sent forward and fired a couple of shells into the retreating Zulus, of whom two having been wounded, Col. Pearson (very anxious to obtain a prisoner for information) sent forward the Native Pioneers[3] to bring them in. In the endeavour to do this much time was lost, and advantage of the delay was taken by the Zulus to recover their surprise and courage, and to commence preparing for cutting off or hindering our retreat. At about 6.45 we commenced our return, and chose a different and longer route. A wise precaution considering the awkward bush.

The RE were ordered to form a right-flank guard in skirmishing order. We again ascended the rising ground and arrived at the kloof we had before visited, in which we were told by the sentry, thrown out by a Company of 99th forming rear guard, were 40 or 50 Zulus. I ordered the Company to get to the edge of the kloof, and, kneeling in the long grass, watch the thick bush, ready to fire by order of officers or section N.C. officers [ie 'ncos']. Immediately we approached the edge of the kloof a couple of shots were fired from the other side of it, one passing, as I thought, pretty close to me. I was conspicuous, being mounted. We waited three or four minutes without seeing anyone in the kloof. I extended the Company still further to the right, and sent the right file to watch the ridge to the right, on the further end of which, about 300 yards off, stood a Kraal. A few shots were exchanged on the right and a volley fired into the kloof by No 2 section, and as it became evident the Zulus had evacuated it, it became a question whether to advance on the Kraal and burn it or return to the Column. The Column having by this time advanced some distance to our front, it seemed to me scarcely safe to run the risk of being cut off from it with a ravine dividing us, so I drew the Company in and presently received an order to join the rear of the Column. We then turned off the road by which we had come to the south-eastward, choosing a more open road over the Veldt, burnt three more Kraals, had a trifling delay in getting the gun over a boggy stream, were followed by Zulus at a very respectful distance and flanked by others, who had evidently hoped to way-lay us, in the bush, on our return home. We fired some shots and two or three shells at these gentlemen with a little effect, ranges 700 to 1,000 yards, and reached the fort without a casualty at 10am. Day very hot; at night I had bad diarrhoea. Determined to manufacture a balloon to gain communication with Natal.'

Night actions were notoriously difficult to carry out. Chances were good of troops getting wildly lost, or of one part of the force losing touch with its comrades, or – potentially disastrously – of confusing friends with enemy. The Zulus had better fieldcraft skills than the Imperial soldiers, and this was their homeland. It was understood that the bayonet was the weapon for night actions: the cold steel charge being far more likely to achieve victory than blind gunfire in the dark. Thus the crucial advantage that the British could boast – their technical superiority – would be set aside for the chancey game of taking on the Zulus by moonlight. It was a calculated risk, for camp security among the Zulus, as with most African peoples, was believed to be fairly rudimentary. Tonight it had worked.

The following day Wynne wrote to Lucy, expanding his account of the attack, and reworking some of the details:-

¶ '2nd March, Sunday – Our expedition came off yesterday, and may be considered a success. We paraded at 2am in the dark, and had to grope along over the 'veldt' (grassy ground) by a track barely visible, past a good deal of thick bush, from which the enemy if he had had (as is usual) his outposts there, might have observed us, given the alarm, and annoyed us with fire which it would have been in vain for us to reply in the dark. We were fortunate however in getting along without apparent observation for nearly the whole way, and as is usual in these latitudes it became very suddenly light when we were within a mile of our destination.

Our force consisted of (in front) 30 Mounted Infantry, then my Company RE, next one 7-pr. gun RA, escorted by the Marines about 40 in number, the four weak companies of the Buffs, the Native Natal Pioneers, some of whom were used as stretcher bearers, as were also the bandsmen of the Buffs, and lastly a company of the 99th Regiment, about 500 in all.

When within three-quarters of a mile of the military kraal (a military kraal is the head-quarters of one or more Zulu regiments, and consists of a number of well constructed wattle and daub huts within a more or less strong enclosure, where the regiments and their 'indunas' or officers live) some of their outposts observed us. The Mounted Infantry were sent to cut them off if possible, but just too late, and my company was extended in skirmishing order to the right front of our column to watch the bush into which they seemed to have entered. After a few minutes we went on, and the RE were sent up a hill through long wet grass to skirmish to the left front of the advancing column. We ascended the hill and crossed it, passing by a deep wooded kloof and then through fields of mealies (or maize) where we came in sight of the military kraal, the object of attack. A shell was fired into the kraal. The Mounted Infantry then advanced upon it, and it was quickly evacuated by the Zulus, who were seen ascending the hills and ridges behind it, driving off their cattle. Others were observed coming from the neighbouring kraals, who dotted themselves upon our right and left front. The Mounted Infantry, and afterwards the Natal Pioneers, then set fire to all the kraals, and the object of the expedition was very simply accomplished, after a few shots at the retreating Zulus.

Two of them having been wounded, and it being considered most desirable to take a Zulu prisoner in order to try and get information out of him, the Natal Pioneers were sent to the front to bring one or both in. They had, owing to the formation of the ground, to make a long detour to get at these wounded men, and after a long and useless delay were unable to find them. Meanwhile our Column did not advance, which was a pity, as there was a second kraal about a mile and a half further on belonging to a gentleman named Dabulamanzi – one of Cetshwayo's brothers, which we might well have destroyed if we had advanced quickly upon it at the first, after destroying the Military kraal (named Esiqwakeni).

Instead of which I fear the Zulus may have thought we did not consider ourselves strong enough to attack the further kraal, though we had intended doing so. After this fruitless delay we started home, and Colonel Pearson wisely chose a different though much longer route – for of course their object now was to waylay us in the bush which skirts the road, and for this our delay had afforded them time.

The RE were ordered to skirmish and form a right flank guard for the retreat. We ascended the hill again and were told that 50 or 60 Zulus[4] were in the deep kloof we had passed before. I brought the men over the crest of the hill and down towards the thick bush of the kloof, cautioning them to watch for the slightest movement in it.

I was the only mounted officer,[5] so probably for me was intended the first shot which came from the opposite slope of the kloof where it curves away changing its direction to one at right angles to our advance. It whizzed past pretty close.

We saw two or three black fellows making away, and as it was useless to descend into this deep kloof one section was ordered to fire a volley into the suspected part of it, but without effect that we could see. Some were seen on a ridge to the right and fired at by a few of our skirmishers, and we would have advanced in their direction and attacked a kraal a short distance off, but that the Column had by this time begun to retire, and we were somewhat left behind. An order was also sent up to me that the RE were to close upon the Column, and follow in rear of the Column of route. I therefore led the company there, and then joined Colonel Pearson's staff. We next advanced towards a largeish kraal belonging to the King, and it was set on fire. Its name is euphonious - 'Kwa, Babangibone.' A little further on another was occupied and burnt. We then came to a slight difficulty in the shape of a very boggy stream, where one's horses legs sank to the hocks. This would not do for the gun – so we had to search further up the stream which wound round out of our course. After a few trials one place seemed less deep, so I called up the Native Pioneers, and made them fetch as much as they could carry of a couple of patches of scrub grass growing near – (there happened to be no brushwood handy) and succeeded in making a passage for the gun. I purpose trying to make something which without being heavy may be carried on these expeditions, and enable the guns to pass over such places without difficulty in future. We had to pass over a small stream, and when we had done so observed the Zulus scattered about in our rear, and on the hills on our right – ie on the opposite side of the Umlalazi – but at long distances. We sent a shell or two into them, and also skirmishing parties to drive them off our flank, which was easily done, and we finally marched into the fort without a single casualty or wound – at 10am, having been at it eight hours.

The sun was very hot on our return, and all day – much more so than it has been for some time. I suppose it was this, and the unwonted exercise (for though I have plenty of work every and all day, I but rarely get away from the fort) that upset me; but I began to feel seedy last night at about six, and had diarrhoea through the night. This morning I found myself weak and headachy, and have been a little miserable all day. I was unable to attend Divine Service with the troops in the open under the hot sun, so I read the Psalms, Lessons, Epistle, and Gospel for the day, at the time, which making allowances for our difference of longitude, I calculated you would be at church. I do so long to be back in civilised life and peaceful times again, with home interests and home service for God, and above all, the congregational services of our Church, with her pure and holy liturgy. If this Zulu War were only over, I would willingly give any officer £150 to exchange with me.[6] But I believe I am wrong to write or think in this way. It is best to leave all things in God's hands, and not to seek to change one's lot or circumstances, unless it be clearly in accordance with the teaching of His word, or the guidance of His Spirit.

This afternoon we were greatly excited by seeing flashing lights[7] from the direction of the Tugela, as if seeking to call our attention. The flashes were strongly visible, but unfortunately, they did not appear to be signalling any message – merely making an occasional flash. We watched for a long time, and endeavoured to flash back in return with ordinary looking glasses and sheets of tin. To-morrow I am going to try and make a fire balloon, ie one with a small reservoir of paraffin and a sponge in it, which being lighted, will keep up the heated rarified air during its passage. The wind is at present blowing directly towards the Lower Tugela, and therefore, favourable. The balloon will be about 6-ft. or 7-ft. high, and 5-ft. in diameter, the little paraffin lamp supported inside by means of a light wire frame, fastened to a wire ring at the bottom. A letter enclosed in some light covering, not inflammable, can be suspended to the bottom, and there is a chance, at least, of its reaching the Natal side of the Tugela, and finally getting into the hands of the General. We shall soon have to take into serious consideration the question of provisions,[8] if we are not relieved before long by the arrival of a convoy. The constant outcry here, especially on Sundays, among most officers, is the want of anything to read (ie, anything of a light description). I certainly should have no time for this kind of reading (if i cared for it) on week days. If I had, I could find much more congenial employment in chatting with you – on paper – even though it may be long enough before it reaches you, if it ever does. I fear however I cannot make myself at all interesting to-night, being in so stupid a state, so good night my darling wife, God bless you.'

It was a long and wide-ranging letter; Wynne may not have been able to send out each of the letters as he completed them, but kept them as part of a one-sided conversation with his wife. In contrast, the Diary for the same day was as sparse as possible:-

¶ 'Sunday, March 2nd – Very seedy, unable to attend Divine Service. Heliograph signals observed in the direction of the Tugela at about 3pm, no message made out. Endeavoured to flash sun's rays back.'

The appearance of British troops on the Tugela brought hope of relief in the next few days. Chelmsford was using a heliograph, operated by Lt Haynes, left behind weeks before in Durban, to open communication. Since there was no corresponding device at Eshowe, every man with a pocket mirror was out on the hillside attempting his own reply. Wynne's response was to plan the building of a balloon to float a message southwards on the wind – an inventive approach, at the very least.

NOTES

1) Dabulamanzi was 35 years old, and commander of the uThulwana regiment. He had led the attack on Rorke's Drift, and would be shot dead by a Boer officer in 1886.
2) The red coats were relics of Isandhlwana, donned by the victorious warriors as part of the ritual that demanded they disembowel slain enemies and themselves undergo purification ceremonies.
3) As speakers of the Zulu language, the Native Pioneers might persuade one or more Zulus to surrender – something that they were hardly likely to do for British regulars.
4) In the Diary the number of Zulus was '40 or 50'.
5) It is not clear that Wynne was the only mounted officer in the whole raiding party, or whether he simply refers to that portion of the force under his direct command. If he was overall the only mounted officer, we might ask 'Why?'.
6) Although the sale of commissions had been abolished, it was still possible for an officer to exchange into another posting – but not while on active service. £150 was, of course, a considerable sum.
7) First reports suggested that the flashing lights indicated that Fort Pearson was on fire.
8) Pearson expected that his force would be able to hold out on the reduced rations until 7th April.

Chapter Eleven: Eshowe IV - A Balloon and a Torpedo

Once the news of Isandhlwana reached the outside world, reaction was swift. The British regulars in Cape Colony – four companies of the 88th on the eastern frontier, and three companies of the 2/4th at Capetown – were rushed to Natal. The 4th arrived at Durban on January 30th, and marched into Pietermaritzburg three days later. The 88th reached Durban on February 8th, having been unwilling to leave the recently pacified borderlands until Volunteers from Capetown had relieved them. Of these four companies, two were sent on to the remnants of the centre company at Pietermaritzburg; one was kept in garrison at the port, and one sent to Stanger to allow men of the 99th already there to move forward to Fort Pearson.

The captain of *HMS Shah* heard the news while docked at St Helena. He decided to override his orders to proceed home from the Pacific, and transported the island garrison – another company of the 88th and an artillery battery – to Natal. They were disembarked, together with 394 bluejackets from the ship's complement, on March 6th.

By 11th February London was aware of the catastrophic events of 22nd January, and quickly determined to squash the Zulus forthwith. Some 10,000 troops were to be sent out, including two regiments of cavalry, six battalions of foot, two batteries and a full array of support services. The first units to arrive were the 57th from Ceylon (11th March); 228 sailors from *HMS Boadicea* (15th March); the 91st Highlanders (17th March), and six companies of the 60th Rifles. This last regiment arrived at Durban on the 20th and was unceremoniously pushed forward, reaching Fort Pearson seven days later.

Until his reinforcements had actually arrived, Lord Chelmsford could do little to retrieve the situation. He spent time – too much time, according to his many critics – on the Inquiry into the Isandhlwana disaster, and in forming the demoralised NNC into five fresh battalions. On 28th February he rode into Fort Pearson, and it was from here that the heliograph made contact with Eshowe.

Wynne's Diary reports the design and creation of his balloon, and of a signalling screen:-

¶ 'March 3rd – No work from 6 to 8am owing to wet. At 9.30 we continued our works as on Friday, same working parties. I commenced constructing a balloon 5' diameter, 6'6' high, to carry a note, enclosed in a small tin case, from Col Pearson to the General, to be inflated by means of a small paraffin lamp in a light wire frame inside it. The balloon was composed of tough tracing paper (vegetable parchment) cut into ten gores, of which the curves were struck with a radius 12'6' to a chord 7.'85 and turned off at the lower end to form the neck. The gores were pasted on to a circular piece of tracing paper divided into ten equal sectors (angle 36°) so as to allow them to overlap by half-an-inch when pasted one over the other. A wire ring was fixed at the mouth of the bottom, and supported by a wire frame holding a small tin cannister with edges turned over, as clips, resting on the wire ring at the top of the frame. The tin cannister contained the paraffin and a piece of sponge, which, when lighted, maintains the rarefaction of the air within the balloon. To-day the signalling from the Tugela was again observed and some words deciphered, of which the import, though vague, seemed to be that a convoy was expected on the 13th inst. with 1,000 men, and that when aware of its approach Col Pearson was to sally out with the surplus of the garrison. This of course caused much excitement and canvassing of the real purport of the message, and many were the endeavours to flash something back with hand mirrors, &c. I determined to try and effect communication by means of a large screen raised above the ground, revolving on horizontal pivots, which being brought alternately to a horizontal and vertical position in front of the place to be signalled to, should produce 'dashes and dots' through the spaces of time of its appearances.'

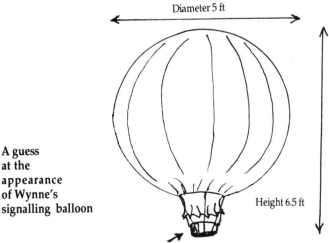

Diameter 5 ft

Height 6.5 ft

A guess at the appearance of Wynne's signalling balloon

Tin with sponge and paraffin lamp, and message tin

¶ 'March 4th – Same work going on; commenced signalling screen. The balloon finished by 4pm. Col Pearson's message in cipher ready by 4.30; we were just preparing to send it up when the sky suddenly became black and threatening, and we determined to reserve it. Very shortly after the rain came, and there was a most severe and prolonged thunderstorm, with torrents of rain during the night.'

The proposed plan, by which Lt Col Law[1] would lead 1,000 troops 'plus natives' to link up with Pearson's force, was optimistic. At this point Chelmsford was hardly in a position to relieve Eshowe. By scraping together the garrisons of Stanger, Pearson and Tenedos (it was too soon for the new arrivals from the Cape), he could amass only five companies of the 99th, two of the Buffs, some bluejackets and Percy Barrow's mounted troops. In face of a Zulu army of unknown – but evidently impressive – numbers, it was a suicidal risk.

Ballooning was one of the areas of military science that fell under the aegis of the Royal Engineers. Observation balloons had been used as early as the French Revolution, at the battle of Fleurus in 1793, and were employed fairly extensively in the American Civil War and the 1870–1 campaign in France. The conservative British establishment, however, was suspicious of any innovation. It was not until the Suakin expedition of 1885 that an RE balloon section, under Major Templer, was to see service. Wynne's ingenuity in devising his tiny balloon probably drew its inspiration from some long-ago lecture at Woolwich; but silk balloons of professional manufacture were highly unreliable. The failure of his improvised dirigible of 'vegetable matter' is scarcely to be wondered at. Beyond this, the continuing bad weather meant that the signalling screen was also to have limited value. The elements, it seemed, were not on the side of 'the red soldiers'.

It was to be Captain MacGregor who resolved the issue, rigging up an improvised heliostat using a pocket mirror and an old iron tube. This allowed two-way contact, although the cloud cover meant that signals could be shut off in mid-sentence, with perhaps hours passing before communication could be resumed. When Col Pearson inquired as to the health of his pregnant wife, the signal reported 'Mrs Pearson is...' and cut off. Several anxious hours later, the heliograph opened up again with: '...well, and delivered of a baby daughter'.

¶ 'March 5th – Continued signalling screen. Left the fort at 1pm with a strong escort of Infantry, under Lt Col Ely, 99th, to make a reconnaissance of a new route towards Inyezane, with a view to shortening the road, and avoiding the bush of the present route. Courtney, Main and Willock accompanied me; we discussed the route and followed it to within a short distance of the proposed junction with the old road, agreed that with not overmuch labour it could be made practicable for waggons, the saving effected in the distance being about five miles. Colonel Pearson on receiving my report determined to have the road commenced without delay. Main caught a fowl in a deserted Kraal.'

If relief were to come, or if the garrison were to make a plunge southwards to meet a force from Natal, the state of the roads would be of great importance. By cutting a new, more direct road towards the Inyezane, not only would several crucial miles be saved on the route, but the dangers of the heavily-forested old trail could be avoided. It was clear that any British advance would be heavily opposed, and there was a serious risk that the bush along the existing road would be the site of a lethal ambush. Wagon roads had to be shallow of gradient, far more so than footpaths: it was an axiom that a draught horse could pull only 64% of its normal load up a I:30 slope; 40% at 1:20, and but 25% at 1:10.[2] With the already overladen wagons employed by the army in Zululand, a steep track could defeat an advance as surely as Cetshwayo's impis.

¶ 'March 6th – Wet from 6 to 8am, no work. Work from 9 to 11am. Usual working parties fetching stone, timber, brushwood, macadamising road; continued huts, put up signalling screen on hill to north of fort, revetted portions of the parapet with sods to replace hurdle revetment, finished sod traverse, south face; filling in pits, south glacis. Intended going out in the afternoon to make a more detailed reconnaissance of the new route towards Inyezane, but prevented by heavy rain. No further signals from Tugela owing to weather.'

Wynne's continued work on the fort suggests that he assumed that the relief of Eshowe would mean a reversion of the fort to its initial role as a stores depot. This would not happen, however, since the site was destined to be abandoned.

¶ 'March 7th – At 7am started for laying out and constructing new road, with Native Pioneers and a Company of Naval Brigade. They worked till driven in by wet at 11am; a large number of Zulus seen in the same direction just before our arrival there. At 9am, I went up to instruct signallers in working the screen, and also to introduce some improvement in the working gear. This and all work about the fort stopped by rain at about 10am. There have been very great hindrances to our work during the last three or four days. At about 10pm I was called up, some Zulus having been noticed on sky line by our sentries about 450 yards distant; fired four shots at the spot where they were just visible; they and others who had approached nearer seen running over the crest of the hill, and disappearing on the other side.'

¶ 'March 8th – At 6am a party of one Company of Buffs and one Company of Naval Brigade left the fort with Main to go on with construction of new road; they were relieved at 8am by one Company 99th, one Company Naval Brigade and Native Pioneers. Rain came on at 10am and continued with strong wind all day. The sides of the communication to caponier, south face, fell in in places last night; the communication was cut out of the solid earth, with strong cross timbers resting on a bearing of 12 to 14 inches. There should have been upright posts at 5' or 6' feet intervals with sills on these on which to fix the cross pieces which carry the parapet above them.

It blew so hard all day that the signalling screen I had put up on the hill was at last broken across by the force of the wind.'

On March 8th Wynne began his first letter to Lucy in a week, written on a section each day since it was clear that no correspondence could be sent out until the siege came to an end.

¶ 'Saturday, 8th March, 1879 – This week has been a very busy one indeed, that is to say we have had a very large number of things on hand to do – and a very disappointing one owing to the hindrances we have met with.

On Monday I was still rather seedy – however, I commenced the balloon and got it half finished. I also commenced making a huge screen of tarpaulin tarred black and stretched on a frame 12ft. by 10ft. which should work on a horizontal axis on two strongly supported uprights. So that when placed on a hill close to the fort it should face the direction of the place from which the flash signalling (*Heliograph*) came, near the Tugela. And by making long and short appearances give the dash (-) and dot (.) from which telegraphic alphabets are formed.[3]

On Monday and Tuesday we descried the heliographic signals and the

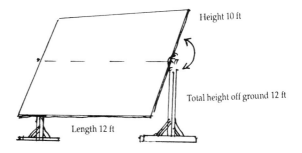

A guess at the appearance of Wynne's signalling screen

Height 10 ft

Total height off ground 12 ft

Length 12 ft

Screen is vertical to expose a 'dot' or 'dash'; horizontal between signals.

following message was made out, though some of the important words were doubtful. 'On or about the 13th, look out for me with a 1,000 men, besides natives, coming by the General's order as far as Inyezane to your support. Sally out with surplus garrison when you become aware of my presence. From Colonel Law, RA to Colonel Pearson.'

There were other words afterwards which could not be made out, and we were anxious to try and communicate with them, so I hurried on the making of the screen, and completed the balloon by 4pm on Tuesday, during the whole of the previous part of which day the wind and weather were most propitious. Colonel Pearson's message was written out in cipher and enrolled in the little tin case, and we were just going to send the balloon up at 4.30, when it suddenly became very threatening with black clouds, and in a few minutes came on to rain, followed by a terrific thunderstorm lasting nearly all night.

The next day the wind was unfavourable, and has continued so with more or less wet weather ever since.

On Wednesday I started with my brother officers here, and an escort of infantry to reconnoitre the ground for two miles or more in the direction of Inyezane (the scene of our fight), with a view to ascertaining if it were not possible to construct a road which should very much shorten the distance, and also avoid the thick bush which lies on either side of the present route, we were fortunate in finding out a line amongst the hills which with a certain amount of excavation would make quite as good a road, if not better than the present one, and at the same time save about five miles or perhaps six, ie two and a-half instead of about eight, which is said to be the distance at present. Next day (it being most important to get the road completed quickly) we were prevented by rain.

The day after only three hours work upon it, and to-day no work at all. The rain has been incessant, and it has blown a hurricane. My poor screen stood the gale till four o'clock in the afternoon, and then broke across and looked a melancholy wreck on the hill.'

¶ 'Sunday, 9th – We had a wet stormy night. The orders were for Divine Service at 7.45am, and working parades at 8.30 and 1.30, to go on with the road; but the weather was so bad that Church Parade was postponed to 4pm, and we could not go to work in the morning. I had to go up the hill to get the remains of the screen, as Colonel Pearson wished for another to be made immediately. In the afternoon at 1.30 we started for the new road, it having cleared up. We were watched by 15 to 20 Zulus, about 800 to 1,000 yards off. They fired at us two or three times, and we returned the compliment. We got a satisfactory afternoon's work done, and returned to the fort at 5.15. I was by this prevented from attending Divine Service. I certainly wish from my heart that this lingering Zulu war were over. It becomes wearisome work, and one has no rest nor time to devote to divine things. If I thought there were a probability of these wars with South African savages recurring frequently – and some people think they will – I should apply for an exchange when this one is over, for it would be inconvenient to have to leave you by yourself out here, and bad financially, having to pay heavy extra premiums for insurance periodically. However, we must hope for the best. Meanwhile I am looking forward to Thursday, when we shall be expecting to leave for the Tugela, and if I get down all right, won't I rush for my letters, which are, I hope, awaiting me there!'

'Sunday, 9th March – It rained and blew hard all last night, and up to near mid-day to-day. Church parade put off till the afternoon. In the morning had to go and fetch down signalling screen with a party of my men and prepare for the construction of a new one. A party of RE also working at caponier communication.

At 1.30pm started with Courtney, Willock, 5 RE, 2 Cos Buffs, 1 Co Naval Brigade and Native Pioneers, to continue the construction of new road to

Inyezane. 15 to 20 Zulus watched us from neighbouring hills, and some shots were exchanged between them and us. We left working at 4.30pm, having made fair progress; soil for good road.'

The precise strength and activities of the Zulus at this time are difficult to gauge. Accounts of Zulu actions between the January battles and the reforming of forces prior to the descent on Evelyn Wood's column at the end of March suggest that most of the army was at its home kraals licking its collective wounds. Captain MacGregor nevertheless believed that there were some 30,000 warriors between Eshowe and Fort Pearson in the early part of March; while Chelmsford's military secretary – John North Crealock – received information that the following regiments were deployed in the Lower Tugela theatre[4]:-

nGobamakosi (6,000)	isaNqu (1,500)	uDhloko (4,000)
uMbonambi (2,000)	Undi corps (c.3,500)	umCijo (9,000)
'Umsikaba' (inSugamgeni? – 1,000)	uNokhenke (2,000)	'Umbelebele' – unidentified.

Theoretical Total: 29,000 (+)

This force was believed to be commanded by Somopho, and there was 'another tribal force at Entumeni under Dabulamanzi'.

Even if these amabutho were not at the full strengths[5] indicated, they formed a clearly formidable host of perhaps 20,000 men. The caution showed by the British – which might at first sight appear unwarranted – is thus entirely understandable.

¶ 'Monday, 10th March – We started at six this morning to continue the making of the new road. The Zulus were on the look-out for us, and gave us annoyance, appearing in large numbers on the neighbouring hills. The covering party of Infantry made a mistake, I thought, in firing at them at long ranges, instead of letting the Zulus waste as much ammunition as they chose, and then if the latter thought fit to come nearer, fire upon them with effect. As it was, the small effect of our infantry fire emboldened the Zulus, and the repeated fire disorganised the infantry working parties, so that it was in vain that we (RE) tried to get them to keep steadily at it. The Zulus finally began to appear in large numbers on our right rear (but at a good distance), and as the cattle were grazing there, Colonel Pearson became anxious, and ordered the whole to retire at about 10am, scarcely any work having been performed. Now, as the road must be completed by the day after to-morrow, this was a sad failure. In the afternoon a much stronger party was sent out, but only a small working party of Native Pioneers, and, to complete the fiasco, not a Zulu was seen. I found it necessary to speak strongly and earnestly on the subject to Colonel Pearson in the evening, saying that I could not be responsible for the completion of the road unless the most vigorous measures were taken during the remaining days, and recommended that to-morrow we should go to the furthest point of the new road, where a stream had to be crossed, rock blasted, etc., and then to work backwards, that a force sufficient to hold its own, under a field officer, should be sent, and that I would not draw upon the Infantry for work, but do it all with the RE and Native Pioneers. I put up a new signalling screen in the afternoon, much stronger than the last, which works well.

A 'runner' arrived from the Tugela with a despatch 14 days old. The despatch was in cipher (Navy code). This man was soon suspected, as his story was not satisfactory. He evidently was sent in by the enemy as a spy, with the despatch taken from one of the runners they murdered. It is now, I think, evident that all our runners since the 11th ult. have failed to reach the Tugela,* and our letters will have been written to no purpose. I wrote you a note on the 11th ult., so I hope you will at any rate get that, though there will be a long gap afterwards.'

*{*One letter, dated February 18th, reached me safely. – L.W.}*

'March 10th – Started at 6am. 1st relief, 2nd party at 7.30am to continue making of road; Zulus gave us some annoyance, appearing in large numbers on neighbouring hills, shots were exchanged between them and our covering parties at absurdly long ranges, and there being no senior officer in recognised command of both covering and working parties, the latter did little or nothing, but were taken off by their officers to reinforce the covering parties. The Zulus worked round to our right flank, though at a considerable distance. Here the cattle, or a portion of them, were grazing, and this fact, together with the sounds of all this random firing, induced Col Pearson to retire the whole at about 10 o'clock; no work to speak of having been done. Time grievously lost, as the day was most favourable. In the afternoon a strong party was sent out besides one gun, the Native Pioneers only working; scarcely a Zulu was seen. A little work only of course was done at the 2nd drift along the road; it was a lost day. A runner arrived in the morning with a letter in cypher from Col Law, RA, to Col Pearson, dated 14 days before. This man told a story of his having been hunted by the Zulus and having fired away all his ammunition, and spoke of himself as belonging to Natal, and in the employment of Mr Finney;[7] he wore a great coat of the 24th Regt. There appeared to be strong grounds for suspecting the truth of his statement, and for believing him to be a spy. In the evening he was handed over to the RE guard to be kept under surveillance.

During the afternoon I put up a new signalling screen, a frame of 12' x 9'6' in the clear, of boards $3^3/_4$ ' x $1^1/_2$ ' set on edge, morticed and braced at the angles with a centre baulk 4' x 3 $^3/_4$ ' into iron sockets (made of $1^3/_4$ ' gas pipes) in which the pins worked loose, which enabled it to revolve. The pins were passed through iron bearings in the upright posts at 12' above the ground; these posts were strutted. The covering for the frame was a tarpaulin, bound all round with a 3' strip of cow hide, punched at every 12' with an eyelet hole to enable the tarpaulin to be laced on the frame when required for use.

We signalled two or three messages to the Tugela signalling station. Signalling from thence was kept up for two or three hours. Weather fine and sunny.

In the evening I spoke earnestly to Col Pearson on the great importance of getting on with the construction of the road, which at the present rate of working could not possibly be finished by the time required.

I induced him to send out to-morrow morning a large party to ensure our getting as far as the junction of the new road with the old, where a drift had to be made.'

Wynne's sickness was becoming ever more debilitating as the month wore on. On 11th March he wrote his last Diary entry; an incomplete sentence tailing off thus:-

¶ 'March 11th – Had an attack of diarrhoea during the night; weak in the morning. Started at 7.30am with...'

Lucy made a note at this point:-

(The Diary ends thus abruptly in the middle of a sentence – L.W.)

Quite why Warren Wynne left off the Diary he had so carefully attended to since January is a mystery. He was sick – sicker than he wanted Lucy to know – but was able to continue his letters to her. Perhaps his diary-letter had taken over the function of the professional journal: perhaps he simply wished to preserve his remaining strength for his wife.

The letter of the 11th completed the story. The 'Torpedo' was an improvised landmine, one of the multitudinous new ways of inflicting harm on others that the scientific 19th century had thrown up. As a sincere Christian, this seems to have concerned Wynne – and certainly he knew it would not sit well with Lucy. His explanation has the hollow ring of the unconvinced, echoing the apologies for novel engines of destruction that have rung down the years to our own time:-

¶ 'March 11th – I had an attack of diarrhoea during the night and was weak at starting on our important expedition this morning. We left at 7.30am and after dropping flanking parties on our right and left, advanced to the point we desired to reach. The Zulus showed along the ridges in front of us, and every now and then shots were exchanged. We worked hard and got the 'drift' made across the stream (this was three miles from the fort). One of the N. Pioneer officers laid a ground torpedo with a long stake immediately over it and connected with it by a string attached to the friction tube, which being pulled would ignite the explosive dynamite. A board, on which was printed in large letters TORPEDO as a warning to Europeans, was nailed to the top of the stake. The Zulus always pull up posts and things of this kind which they suppose we have put up for our assistance. We had not long left the spot when a tremendous explosion was heard and some Zulus seen rushing off as if in terror. If there were many on the spot at the time there must have been havoc made among them. These things seem nasty and cruel, but that is just what war is , and if they help to shorten the period of war they have something in their favour.

We then marched back three-quarters of a mile to where two other drifts had to be made, one through a marsh, the other through a stream with rocky bed. It was then 11 o'clock or near it. These places lay in a valley with hills rising on every side, the sun very hot – I began to feel it, but there was no time to think. We cut out the marshy ground and filled in with brushwood, and then started blasting at the rocky bed, and by the use of large heavy stones, not likely to be carried away, well bedded in and protected on the up stream side by heavy timbers stretched across, we made an even causeway, which, with a covering of sods, ought to enable heavy waggons to pass over satisfactorily. More of the road was excavated, and altogether we did a good day's work. Unhappily one officer was wounded, but as his escape was wonderful, it is perhaps a matter rather for congratulation. The bullet struck him on the temple and then simply grazed the skin round towards the back of his head. Indeed, I believe it was only a slug.[8] He is considered to be in no danger.

There is, I am sorry to say, a good deal of sickness in the fort. We have lost over a dozen men and one officer.'

NOTES

1) Col Francis Towry Adeane Law, RA, had served on the Court of Inquiry after Isandhlwana, and was presently commander of the Lower Tugela District. He would lead a brigade during the relief of Eshowe in April.
2) Cited in Wolseley, op cit, p 330
3) Two 'telegraphic alphabets' were in use – the Morse code, and a naval cypher which used a different sequence of dots and dashes for the symbols.
4) Letter from Crealock to Maj Gen Sir Archibald Alison CB, 19th March 1879, cited in Clarke, *Zululand at War*, op cit p 152.
5) The full regimental strengths are from Ian Knight, *There Will Be An Awful Row* ,op cit, pp 43–4.
6) Lucy noted that the letter of 18th February had reached her safely.
7) H Bernard Fynney was a border agent, administrator and amateur ethnologist. He wrote a short survey of the Zulu army that was issued to Chelmsford's officers before the campaign.
8) The Zulus, like many African peoples, were badly supplied with ammunition, and would use bits of lead, nails, stones &c, instead. These improvised bullets did not fit the bore of their weapons, and so had little 'stopping power'.

Chapter Twelve: Camp Tugela - A Death in Zululand

Warren Wynne's final letters to his wife dwelt on the fever that wracked his body. For days he had been driving himself on, disregarding his physical illness, to continue his work. The coastal region of Zululand and Natal had a reputation for pestilence, especially in contrast to the cooler, healthier air of the upland Veldt. Surgeon-General Woolfrye[1] compiled a medical report immediately after the war; in it he referred to the 'sea fever' – beginning in February and continuing through May, with its peak in March – allegedly caused by the prevailing north-easterlies blowing 'the miasma of the St Lucia swamps' towards Natal. Dysentery and Enteric Fever – ie Typhoid – were increasing in Eshowe

¶ '13th March – The night before last my rest was much disturbed after the hot day's work, and at 5am I had a bad attack of diarrhoea up to the time when I had to start for the new road. I was standing about laying out a new piece, the morning was rather chilly, and I suddenly felt shivery and found it necessary to walk back to the fort. I went to the hospital and asked to see Dr Norbury, the principal medical officer, but as he was out, another surgeon, after a cursory glance, gave me a chalk powder, which I knew better than to take. I went to my waggon, feeling by this time very ill, burning head, aching eyeballs, chilled skin and aching bones. I took some drops of sal volatile, lay down and covered myself over with all I could muster. (By the way, I have treated myself homeopathically hitherto, and I think with good results tell dear old Andrew. How I wish I could meet him as of yore, at the end of his day's work, waiting for him at the gate to walk with him, and have one of our enjoyable chats on his way home.) After a little time, as I grew worse, I sent for Dr Norbury, who told me to have a piece of linen wet with brandy and water constantly over my forehead and temples. The hot sun and walking across the streams, getting my feet and legs wet above the knees, and the early morning chill, were enough to knock over such an unfortunate being as I am, as regards physique. I was feverish with splitting headache all day yesterday. I am, of course, greatly pulled down, but the fever is gone, and I feel already brighter.

The worst of it was that this was the day we were warned by a signal to be ready to start for the Tugela, and I was in such fear that I should not be allowed to go, though I was determined to do so if possible.

To-day, however, a message has been received to the following effect:-

'Relief postponed till 1st April, when convoy with 4,000 and 2,000 natives will start. Garrison and all waggons will retire; 60th Rifles will replace you *********** (message lost) and 57th are already landed. 15th Transports and 8,000 troops of all arms are on the way.'

This was satisfactory in one way, in that it means a general advance instead of a partial retreat, as our move down would have been; moreover we should certainly have been attacked by very large forces of the enemy, who know all our intended movements through spies etc., and we should have probably lost men, and also have had others laid up from inability to make long marches. But it seems hard that this column, which has borne the burden and heat of the day so far, should be condemned to go back, and not to advance to the certain victory.

Perhaps the 'Garrison' in the message will not include the RE. It is, however, joyful news to hear of so many troops coming to settle this business quickly, for now there will be a chance of our meeting at an earlier date than I had feared we should. Perhaps July or August may see you out here with the precious chicks. That indeed, seems a long long way off, but all is ordered for our good if we use it rightly.

I wonder how Arthur is getting on in Afghanistan. The whole of Europe might be revolutionised, for any chance we have of hearing news.

Colonel Pearson has been most kind in enquiring and coming to see me while I was ill these two days. He has throughout been most cordial and very considerate to me during a trying time which I have had here.

My back is getting wearied and my head stupid, so I must leave off for to-night.

God bless you my precious wife, and you my sweet bairns.'

Fleet-Surgeon H F Norbury, of *HMS Active*, worked tirelessly. His hospital in the mission church was continually overflowing with patients, and medical stores soon gave out. He turned to the contents of the veterinary supplies, and finally to creating his own cures from herbs, plants and tree-bark... some of which proved surprisingly effective. Even the best physician, however, could not succeed without medicines – and so Norbury sent two Africans to make the dangerous run for British-held territory to bring back supplies. They returned on 29th March with drugs, and a package of British newspapers:-

¶ '14th March – I had a most disturbed night last night, I could not sleep except by short snatches, and my brain went working upon what is before us to do here. When I did go off I had horrid nightmares. The waggons were going helter skelter along our new road, tumbling over the embankments, while I was pursued by Zulus five times magnified in the midst of the fracas. In the morning I felt certainly not so well as the day before, nor do I seem to have made any improvement.

I am afraid I am a useless individual to send soldiering, too bad a bargain for Her Majesty to pay for?

I had better go home after this is over and get my retiring annuity, and then become a Schoolmaster, or an Insurance Agent, or Tax Collector. Ask Messrs. D - E - and B - if they could give me employment as Assistant-Master. I would give drill gratis! We have now about 23 days longer to remain here, I should think. I hope I shall at any rate pluck up within that time, but from past frequent experience I cannot have much absolute certainty of it, especially under these circumstances. I have been drawing a plan for huts and have made my head, eyes and back ache, so I think I had better close this for the present. Good night, darling wife, God bless you.'

¶ 'Sunday, 16th – I intended to have written a little yesterday, but after a short stroll of 400 or 500 yards, was so tired that I became lazy. The night before last I had a good night's rest, and was somewhat better in the morning in consequence. Towards evening the livery symptoms returned with something of a fever, and I had a very restless night. Nothing could be kinder than Colonel Pearson, our Commandant. In the morning he comes or sends to enquire, and in the course of the day sits with me and chats. Yesterday both morning and afternoon he sat with me an hour at a time. I told him I was beginning to fear that my present low state of health (for it has now been going down three or four weeks) might disable me from taking an active part in the future of the Campaign. We had just heard by heliograph of Courtney's promotion, and he had said 'we must make you a

Local Major, however your brevet will soon give you that title', and though I never cared to count beforehand upon such things, I should then lose all chance of it. He answered 'Why you are sure of it already.' We were given an opportunity to-day for the first time, of 'giving unto the Lord' at Divine Service. Of course I could not attend the parade, but I sent my contribution over night to Mr Robertson, the Chaplain. The money will probably be given in aid of the wives and families of men who have died in the Campaign, and other such purposes.

We heard yesterday by heliograph, that the 91st Regiment had landed. The quicker they all come the better. It is quite evident the Zulus receive accurate information of all our intended movements, and as they can move so rapidly from place to place (a large force 40 or 50 miles a day) they gain immense advantages. Yesterday it was estimated that 20,000[2] of them were passing by us in a N.W. direction from the other side of the Inyezane, where they had evidently gathered in order to oppose our originally intended march to the Tugela on the 13th and following days.

Dr Norbury thought I was somewhat better, but the liver still out of order, and unfortunately, he had none of the medicine needed to set it right. The authorities were very remiss on this point in sending a very short supply of medicines, and it is worse and worse now that we have stayed here so much longer than was anticipated. Whether nature will set things right if left to herself or not remains to be seen.'

By the 28th March Captain MacGregor reported that 3 officers and about 22 men had died, and that 'about 90 or 100 are regularly attending hospital'.[3] The first to die was Captain John Mainwaring Williams, aged 40, of the Buffs. He passed away on the 12th. On the 16th young Midshipman Cadwallader Coker died – he had insisted on sleeping in the open next to his much-beloved Gatling gun, and exposure to the rains brought on dysentery. Wynne's trial was to last rather longer:-

¶ '17th March – I had not such a good day yesterday. Felt nausea and was feverish in the afternoon and evening. Colonel Pearson came and sat with me for a while, morning and afternoon. He is most kind. I was so glad to hear from him that they had heliographed that Mrs Pearson and his children were quite well.

I am very anxious to know whether it is intended that my Company should retire with the rest of the garrison. Unless they are sending out more RE from England it is doubtful if they can spare us, or at any rate all. Then comes the question as to whether after this pulling down of my strength, unless I quickly get up again, I shall be properly fit for the march – for they intend going without tents, and the extremes of heat by day and cold by night are very great as our winter comes on. The men of the Company have suffered considerably, 50 per cent. are really not fit for marching and bivouac work. I am sorry to say we lost an Officer, RN, and three men in hospital last night. The death list is becoming considerable.

They heliographed to us yesterday the news that peace had probably been concluded in Afghanistan, which I was glad to hear for it will bring Arthur home soon I hope...'

The letter stopped at this point. Lucy made a note:-

[There the letter ends abruptly. On the last two days it had evidently been written with great difficulty and in much weakness. – L. W.]

She continued:-

¶ 'On the 23rd April, 1879, exactly a week after we had heard the news of the relief of Eshowe, the first tidings of my husband's illness reached us, in a telegram to me from Capt. Courtney, RE, dated from the Tugela River on the 7th April, saying: 'Capt. Wynne seriously ill – when able to be moved will be invalided home.' Then came a week of terrible anxiety – and then – the knowledge, merely known officially, that on his birthday, the 9th April, he had passed away from this world. There were yet some days of waiting before any details reached us, and then came the following most kind letter from Capt. Courtney to my father,[4] with my husband's own unfinished letter from Eshowe:-

¶ 'Camp, Tugela, 10th April, 1879 – Dear Sir, I very greatly regret to have to inform you that Capt. Wynne's illness terminated fatally yesterday evening at eight o'clock. His illness commenced at Eshowe on the 11th March, when he had an attack of diarrhoea, but he did not give up working till the 12th. I do not know how far his letters (that I send with this) extend, but I am pretty sure that he never wrote anything after 13th March. He had a very bad attack of continued fever, from which he rallied slightly, but towards the end of March congestion of the lungs came on, and when we evacuated Eshowe, on the 4th of April, and it became necessary to move all the sick, this disease was still on him. We made him as comfortable as we could for the journey on a framework of strips of hide, on which his mattress rested, so as to ease as much as possible the frightful jolting on these bad roads. The doctor told him that moving would be bad for him but he (Capt. Wynne) said that even if he had the choice he would prefer to risk the journey. We had fine weather for the march, and he arrived here about 8.30am on Monday, 7th April, and was at once sent over to the hospital, on the high ground on the other side of the river, near Fort Pearson. The doctor here pronounced his case the worst of those sent down from Eshowe. I was not with him when he arrived, but Lieut. Haynes, RE, who commanded a detachment here, gave him his letters, and he took food; in fact, he did not seem to be at all the worse for the journey. By the doctor's advice I sent a telegram which should reach Mrs Wynne via Cape and Madeira, on the 25th April or thereabouts. I saw him again on Tuesday afternoon, when he gave me some directions about closing up the Company accounts, and asked for my wife's address in England. He has dozed the greater part of the day for a long time past, and has also been very deaf from the amount of quinine he has taken (I presume), so that it was an effort to him to talk. He also directed me to send a telegram to Mrs Wynne, with the words 'I am coming' only. Yesterday, most unfortunately, I was detained in camp all day by business, all the other officers RE being away on duty, and I was unable to pay him my afternoon visit. The doctor was over here, and told me that a bad symptom had set in, viz, bleeding under the skin, and that he did not expect him to linger more than two days. He did not advise subjecting him to the shock of being told that his end was so near, but he said that I should ask him if his affairs were arranged.

I fully intended to have paid him an afternoon visit and asked him if he wished anything attended to, but I was detained too late, and most bitterly do I regret it. He had a corporal whom he liked in constant attendance upon him, and he tells me that he slept almost all day, only waking to take food. Another Engineer Officer, Lieut. Willock (who was in the same marquee, with a slighter attack of fever) was beside him, and, about 8pm, they noticed that his breathing ceased, and he was found to have passed away. He had no pain, and I know that he was quite prepared for another world.' ...

...'His work at Eshowe will not soon be forgotten, and the enclosed extract from his diary will show that the stand made there was mainly due to his advice. That stand has cost him his life humanly speaking, and he has died a soldier's death, as truly as any man ever did. I have been under fire with him twice, and he was always cool and collected. He was only too devoted to his work, and on the 11th of March, the morning after the attack he mentions in his diary, he had a walk of six miles and more in the hot sun, and I fear we must attribute his illness partly at least to this. Of course he had to bear the hardships of the Campaign, and short rations, and all combined, have proved too much for him.' ...

NOTES

1) Cited in the *Précis of Information*.
2) Wynne's report of 20,000 Zulus moving northwest – towards Cetshwayo's designated rendezvous at onDini – dovetails with MacGregor's and Crealock's estimates of very large numbers of warriors in the Lower Tugela area early in March. The Zulu army that assembled and marched west to attack Evelyn Wood at Kambula on March 29th was estimated at 20–25,000 strong.
3) MacGregor, in *Zululand at War*, p 150.
4) It is an interesting piece of Victorian etiquette that David Courtney chose to write to Captain Parish rather than to his daughter – the widow of Captain Wynne.
5) 2nd Corporal J Robinson, RE.

The Battle of Gingindhlovu and the Relief of Eshowe

Lord Chelmsford arrived to take command of the relief expedition, then assembling on the lower Tugela, on 23rd March. The total force amounted to 3,390 Europeans and 2,280 Africans – the most considerable army yet seen under the British flag in Southern Africa. Chelmsford had taken careful note of the most obvious blunders in his previous campaign. The column was to travel light, without tents. It took with it only 122 wagons and carts, which by South African standards was a minimum level of wheeled transport. The idea was also to entrench each afternoon in a wagon-laager surrounded by a shelter trench for the infantry. Security was the watchword.

In two brigades, the force crossed the river into Zululand at daybreak on the 29th. As part of the bid for afety a more easterly route through open country was taken, rather than Pearson's original approach. Heavy rain during the previous two days meant that progress was slow. The column laagered each day on the south bank of a river – the Inyoni on the 29th and the Amatikulu on the 30th. Crossing the swollen Amatikulu took most of the next day; then on 1st April the relief expedition advanced towards the Inyezane. Large parties of Zulus had been seen by the scouts. About noon the column halted on a low ridge a mile south of the river, close to the kraal of Gingindhlovu burned by Pearson's men ten weeks before. The country was free of bush but cloaked in elephant grass. John Dunn, the experienced frontier settler who had tried to avoid involvement in the war, was leading his own retainers as scouts, but chose to make a personal reconnaissance as dusk fell. He returned with the word that a sizeable impi was encamped beyond the river. The camp fires flickered across the Inyezane that night, as rain fell steadily. Dawn brought a heavy mist. Shortly before 6am the vedettes reported that the Zulus were advancing, and within minutes the impi could be seen from the laager.

The Zulu army, commanded by Somopho, consisted of 10–12,000 warriors. These were the units beaten at Inyezane in January, together with irregulars from the coastal Tonga clans, and elements from the uThulwana, uMbonambi, umCijo, nGobamakosi and uVe. This force had been drawn up to cover the relief expedition while the bulk of Cetshwayo's army was withdrawn to assault Wood's entrenchments at Kambula.

Chelmsford's army was as follows[1]:-

57th Regiment	640
91st Regiment	850
6 coys 3/60th	570
2 coys 2/3rd & 5 coys 99th, total:	570
Combined Mounted Inf & Volunteers	430
Naval Brigade (incl 100 marines):	c.350
4th & 5th batalions NNC, total:	2,280
2 x 9 pounder guns RA	
4 x 24 lb rocket tubes	
2 x Gatling guns	

Somopho had been instructed to attack the column on the march, strung out over several miles. British caution, however, had stifled any opening for an ambush. Now he detached a reserve of some 2,000 men and launched his remaining regiments towards the laager from the west and north-west. Once again, however, the impetuous dash of the Zulus wrecked the co-ordination of the assault. The left horn swung to become a pair of wings, crossing the river and charging towards the north and east faces of the entrenchment. Behind them – crucial minutes behind – the centre and right came over the brow of Umisi Hill, mingling together as they approached the west and south faces. Captain Edward Hutton of the 3/60th recalled the sight of the Zulu attack:

Map 8 - The Battle of Gingindlovu, 2nd April 1879

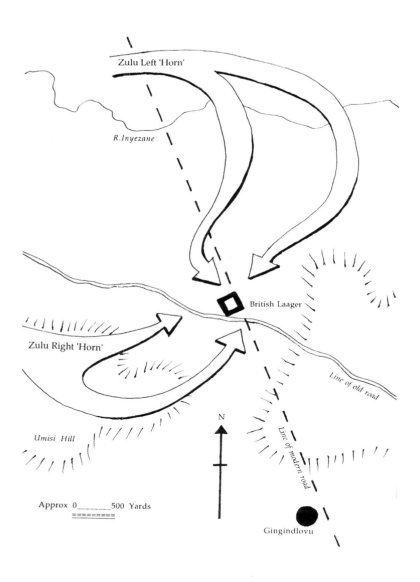

Zulu Left 'Horn'

R.Inyezane

British Laager

Zulu Right 'Horn'

Line of old road

Umisi Hill

N

Line of modern road

Approx 0_____500 Yards

Gingindlovu

'A small knot of five or six would rise and dart through the long grass, dodging from side to side with heads down, rifles and shields kept low and out of sight. They would then sink suddenly into the long grass, and nothing but puffs of curling smoke would show their whereabouts'.[2]

The assault, however, was caught on the section volleys of Martini fire. The Zulus could charge from cover, but none were able to press their charge closer than 50 yards from the laager. The offensive spirit of Isandhlwana and Rorke's Drift was somehow absent. By 6.45 the Zulus were beginning to retreat, their ardour fading fast. Chelmsford sent Barrow's horsemen in pursuit, followed by the suddenly-heroic NNC. For two miles the victors hacked down the fleeing warriors. Zulu losses were about 1,100 men, while the British lost but 13 killed and 48 wounded.

The relief of Eshowe was something of an anticlimax. Colonel Pearson held fast at the fort while the distant sound of action at Gingindlovu could be heard to the south east. Lord Chelmsford spent the remainder of the day resting his men, then completed the march to Eshowe on the 3rd. The first man into the fort was a correspondent, C L Norris-Newman of *The Standard*, who raced ahead and galloped through the gates shouting 'First in Eshowe!'. The formal entry was led by the pipes of the 91st Highlanders. Then the fortifications, so carefully built by Captain Wynne, were hastily demolished and the site abandoned. There was a brief, unsuccessful attempt to capture Dabulamanzi; then the long column marched back south towards the Tugela. Behind the retreating troops, the Zulus set light to Fort Eshowe.

References

1) These strengths are derived from the official Narrative p 63, and from C L Norris-Newman, *In Zululand with the British* (London, 1880) p 137. Two brigades were formed, under Lt Col Law, RA, and Lt Col Pemberton, 3/60th – but command of the entrenched laager was exercised directly by Lord Chelmsford.
2) Emery, *The Red Soldier*, op cit, p 200.

Postscript - Remembrance

Warren Wynne died on his 36th birthday, April 9th 1879; the Wednesday before Easter. He left behind a wife, Lucy Parish Wynne, and sons aged five years, two years and seven months.

A section of Lucy's memoir of her husband is devoted to the letters she received after his death. Several of them are from Courtney and other soldiers serving in Zululand as the war came to its end. Most of them were concerned to relate reassuring details of Wynne's last days. Captain Courtney promised to get a photograph of the grave site on Euphorbia Hill; while Lt Haynes made a sketch of the site and sent it on 22nd April. Harry Willock, stricken with fever and invalided home himself, wrote from his family home in Tenby, North Wales, that '...I remember his pleasure at getting his letters, and reading them through. His end was quiet, and I think I may say without any pain.'[1] The Reverend Robertson told how he had read aloud from a favourite book of Wynne's, *Homeward Bound* by the Rev F E Paget, and that 'He was very patient, and resigned to whatever might be God's will regarding him.'[2] Colonel Pearson, recovering from typhoid, wrote from the Officers' Hospital at Durban on June 19th:-

¶ 'Dear Mrs Wynne – Before I say anything else, let me assure you how truly I feel for you in your bereavement. The sudden, and I suppose quite unexpected news of your poor husband's death must have shocked you terribly. This has indeed been *a widow-making war*, [My emphasis, H.W.] and it makes one's heart bleed to reflect what misery and sorrow it has spread through the land.

Dear Mrs Wynne, your husband and I had been acquainted only a very short time, but in that time I learnt to esteem him very much for his sterling qualities, both as a man and a soldier,and I had hoped that we should never again have lost sight of each other. Before he got ill, I used often to go and chat with Wynne in his waggon. He lived in a tented waggon. We generally began on business matters, and then drifted off to other subjects. His Fort at Eshowe is apparently now quite an historical work, and he and his men did not leave a stone unturned to make the entrenchment perfect. For a long time after he really was too ill to work, Wynne would insist upon remaining at his duty, contrary to the advice of us all. At last, however, he had to give in, and in a very few days I was grieved to learn from the Surgeon that his health was in a most precarious state. We had him transferred from his waggon to a tent, and I used at first to go and sit with him, but latterly, whenever I went to the tent I generally found him in a doze. Of course the journey from Eshowe to Tugela did not tend to improve him, and only three days, I think, after our arrival he died. Poor fellow, he is buried in the cemetery we constructed near Fort Pearson, at the Lower Tugela. Again begging you to accept my most sincere sympathy,

Believe me, dear Mrs Wynne, Yours sincerely, C K Pearson.'

Most of the letters of consolation are of a conventional Victorian kind, rich in sentiment and altogether far too flowery for modern tastes. Lucy recorded that she included the extracts in order to 'shew to my children how their dear father was loved, respected, and valued by all who knew him - in whatever relationship they stood to him.' Several are from officers expressing the belief that, had he lived, Wynne 'would have returned covered with well earned honours,'[3] and that his future would have been bright. Two are from NCOs in the 2nd Field Company, respectfully asking permission of their commanding officer's widow to offer their condolences. More are from clergymen, heavy with allusions to Wynne's place as a 'true soldier of the cross,'[4] and praising his unselfish gifts of time and effort to the benefit of others. We can today perhaps glimpse an unconscious irony in the eulogy from the Reading Parish Magazine:-

¶ 'He is one of the many victims of the critical struggle between barbarism and civilisation, heathenism and Christianity, on the result of which, the future of South Africa depends...'[5]

Lucy Wynne was concerned to make a positive assessment of her husband's service in South Africa, probably to assure her sons that their father had not died in vain, performing merely minor duties in the wilderness of savage Africa. A part of the original introduction was devoted to this:-

¶ 'So that to Captain Wynne is in no small degree it was due that Fort Eshowe was held, and a firm front shown to the Zulu forces for so many weeks, when a retreat to the Tugela Mouth would have involved a deplorable loss of prestige to the British arms, and invited that invasion of Natal which it was the first object to prevent, and which another gallant Engineer Officer, Major Chard, had so effectively checked on the Buffalo River.

This view is confirmed by Colonel Pearson, who, in his despatch, wrote as follows:

¶'Personally I was in favour at first of retiring; but on further reflection, I judged that if we continued to hold the forward position in the country, nearly forty miles from the frontier, it might have a good moral effect, and even afford protection to that part of the Colony immediately behind.' – And Lord Chelmsford wrote in his despatch of the 10th April, 1879: 'I am much indebted to Colonel Pearson for so tenaciously holding on to Eshowe, after the bad news of the Isandhlwana affair had reached him. The occupation of that Fort... had, no doubt, a very powerful moral effect throughout South Africa.'

In the course of a speech made at Yeovil, shortly after his return to England, Colonel Pearson said: - 'I have been given credit for my skill in rendering our fort at Eshowe impregnable, but it was made so by Captain Wynne, my Commanding Engineer, and his brother officers, under whose directions we all worked. Captain Wynne died of an illness brought on by exposure, and by unflinchingly remaining at his duty when almost incapable of performing it.'

A modern review of Wynne's service suggests that Lucy was right to applaud his contribution to the successful defence of Eshowe, and the significance of that defence to the course of the campaign. Certainly the holding of the advanced post in Zulu territory did much to suggest that, despite the catastrophe of Isandhlwana and the resulting collapse of British morale and reputation, the war was far from lost. What we know of Cetshwayo's plans indicate that he did not entertain notions of overrunning Natal anyway – but this was by no means apparent at the time. Wynne was vocal in his support of retaining Fort Eshowe; he was inventive in planning the defensive works, and tireless in their execution. His imagination was constantly at work. Others wondered at the constancy of his efforts, and more than one writer suggested that overwork was the fundamental cause of his death. Wynne showed a naïveté – a boyish enthusiasm – that resulted in frequent self-doubt which helped him to redouble his efforts, especially as he pitched headlong into the first days off the campaign. His comrades and subordinates responded with devotion. Of the pieces in the memoir, the most affecting is part of a letter written by Corporal Garner of Wynne's company, to his own wife:-

¶ 'I told you in my last that Captain Wynne was dead. He died the day after we marched into Tugela Camp. It will be sad news for his wife and family.

Every man in the Company deeply regrets his death. I can safely say there is not a man but would do anything for him, he was so respected by them.

It was a sad sight to see our men standing over his grave with tears in their eyes. Capt Courtney was the only officer present, the others being up country, but he was so deeply cut up he could hardly read the Burial Service.'

The 2nd Field Company served throughout the remainder of the Zulu War, with Courtney in command.

An announcement appeared in the London Gazette on 5th May 1880:- 'Captain Warren Richard Colvin Wynne, Royal Engineers, to be Major, in recognition of his distinguished services during the Zulu Campaign, 1878 –79. Dated 2nd April, 1879. Since deceased.' At this period there was no allowance for posthumous decoration, but on the same day a letter was sent to Lucy from the War Office. It confirmed the majority for Warren Wynne, and went on to state that 'In consideration of the distinguished services rendered by him in the defence of Eshowe, the Secretary of State for War has been pleased to award you a special pension of £100 a year, in lieu of £65, of which you are now in receipt &c &c.'

Lucy was concerned to ensure that the gravesite *(See Frontispiece)* was properly tended, recording that H Bernard Fynney, the administrator and border agent, had written on 1st November 1880, that–

¶ 'Brevet Major Wynne's grave has a rail fence round it, and is at present protected. The grave is clear from weeds, and the rose bushes planted are growing well.'

Lucy added that:-

'There was erected at my Husband's grave in September, 1879, a cross of dark grey stone, with the following inscription round the sides of the three stone steps on which it stands:-

In loving memory of
Warren Richard Colvin Wynne
Captain, RE, CRE at Ekowe
Died at Fort Pearson, Tugela, on his birthday, April 9th, 1879,
of fever, contracted during the defence of Ekowe.
Aged 36

I believe in the Resurrection of the body and the life everlasting.
Them that sleep in Jesus will God bring with Him.
He is not dead, but sleepeth.
Christ's faithful soldier and servant unto his life's end.
Dulce et decorum est pro patria mori'

The gravesite may still be seen, at the Euphorbia Hill cemetery, overlooking the River Tugela and the remains of Fort Tenedos, which was built by Warren Wynne in January, 1879.

NOTES

1) Letter of 16th July 1879
2) Letter of 10th May 1879
3) Colonel Grant DAG, RE, 'Horse Guards, War Office, May 9th 1879'
4) The Rev N T Garry, Vicar of Reading
5) Issue for July 1879

Bibliography

(See also the bibliographical commentary contained in the 'Editor's Foreword', above)

Michael Barthorp, *The Zulu War, a Pictorial History*, (Poole, Dorset, 1980)

Ian Castle and Ian Knight, *Fearful Hard Times* (Greenhill, London 1994)

Daphne Child, ed, *The War Journals of Colonel Henry Harford CB* , (Pietermaritzburg, 1978)

David Clammer, *The Zulu War* , (London, 1973)

Sonia Clarke, *Invasion of Zululand*, (Johannesburg, 1979)

Sonia Clarke, *Zululand at War*, (Johannesburg, 1984).

Christopher J Duffy, *Fire and Stone, the science of fortress warfare 1660–1860*, (London, 1975)

Frank Emery, *The Red Soldier – Letters from the Zulu War, 1879* , (London, 1977)

Frank Emery, *Marching Over Africa* , (London, 1986)

Hon Gerald French, *Lord Chelmsford and the Zulu War* , (London 1939)

The Royal Engineers' Journal

J J Guy, *The Destruction of the Zulu Kingdom* , (Bristol, 1979)

Arthur Harness, *The Zulu Campaign* (in Fraser's Magazine, March 1880; partially reprinted in *Invasion of Zululand*, op cit, pp 92–3)

The Intelligence Division of the War Office, *Narrative of the Field Operations connected with the Zulu War of 1879* , (London, 1881)

The Intelligence Division of the War Office, *Précis of Information Concerning Zululand*, (Several editions up to 1895)

Ian J Knight, ed, *There Will Be An Awful Row At Home About This* , (The Victorian Military Society, London, 1979, revised 1987)

Ian J Knight, *Brave Men's Blood* (Greenhill, London 1990)

Ian J Knight, *The Zulus* , (Osprey edition, London, 1989)

J P C Laband and P S Thompson, *Field Guide to the War in Zululand and the Defence of Natal* , (University of Natal, Pietermaritzburg, 1979, revised 1983)

J P C Laband and P S Thompson, *Fight Us in the Open* , (University of Natal, Pietermaritzburg, 1985)

Lt Wilfrid Lloyd, RA, *The Siege of Eshowe* , (London, 1881)

Angus McBride, *The Zulu War* , (London, 1978)

MacGregor, *Zululand at War* , (Manuscript reprinted in Clarke's *Zululand at War*, op cit, pp 148 ff.)

J P MacKinnon and S H Shadbolt, *The South African Campaign of 1879* , (London, 1882)

D F C Moodie, *The History of the Battles and Adventures of the British, the Boers and the Zulus &c in Southern Africa* , (2 Vols, London, 1888)

Donald R Morris *The Washing of the Spears* , (London, 1966)

Fleet-Surgeon Henry Norbury,*The Naval Brigade in South Africa during the years 1877–78–79* , (London, 1880)

C L Norris-Newman, *In Zululand with the British* , (London, 1880)

Howard Whitehouse, *Battle in Africa 1879–1914* , (Fieldbooks, Camberley, 1988)

Sir Garnet Wolseley, *The Soldier's Pocket Book for Field Service* , (3rd edn, London, 1874)